50 Life Skills to Ensure Kids Stay In School,
Off Drugs and Out of Trouble

Also available from Network Continuum:

Emotional Intelligence and Enterprise Handbook – Cheryl Buggy
Future Directions – Diane Carrington and Helen Whitten
Learning to Learn for Life – Rebecca Goodbourn, Steve Higgins, Linda Siegle, Kate Wall and Julia Wright
Learning to Learn for Life 2 – Rebecca Goodbourn, Steve Higgins, Suzie Parsons and Julia Wright
Toon Cards: A Multi Purpose Resource for Developing Communication Skills – Chris Terrell

50 Life Skills to Ensure Kids Stay In School, Off Drugs and Out of Trouble

David Becker

network
continuum

Continuum International Publishing Group
Network Continuum
The Tower Building   80 Maiden Lane
11 York Road   Suite 704
London   New York
SE1 7NX   NY 10038

www.networkcontinuum.co.uk
www.continuumbooks.com

© David Becker 2008

All rights reserved. No part of this publication may be reproduced or transmitted in any form or by any means, electronic or mechanical, including photocopying, recording, or any information storage or retrieval system, without prior permission in writing from the publishers.

David Becker has asserted his right under the Copyright, Designs and Patents Act, 1988, to be identified as Author of this work.

British Library Cataloguing-in-Publication Data
A catalogue record for this book is available from the British Library.

ISBN: 9781855394612 (paperback)

Library of Congress Cataloguing-in-Publication Data
Becker, David.
 50 life skills to ensure kids stay in school, off drugs and out of trouble / David Becker.
   p. cm.
 Includes bibliographical references.
 ISBN 978-1-85539-461-2
 1. Children--Life skills guides. 2. Life skills--Study and teaching--Activity programs. 3. Juvenile delinquency--Prevention.
 4. Parenting. I. Title. II. Title: Fifty life skills to ensure kids stay in school, off drugs and out of trouble.

 HQ781.B367 2008
 649'.7--dc22

2008019545

Illustrations by Grant Devlin
Typeset by Free Range Book Design & Production Limited
Printed and bound in Great Britain by MPG Books, Cornwall

AUGUSTANA LIBRARY
UNIVERSITY OF ALBERTA

'Tell me and I forget
Teach me and I remember
Involve me and I learn. '

Benjamin Franklin

For my children,
Taylor and Summer

ABOUT THE AUTHOR

David Becker is an internationally qualified lawyer with a degree in psychology who was inspired by his forays into the field of personal development and character education. Over the past 20 years, David has studied and trained with some of the world's leaders in personal development and character education, such as Tony Robbins, Deepak Chopra, Randy Gage, Tony Buzan and Mike Dooley.

After graduating from leading peak performance coach Anthony Robbins' Mastery University, David specialized in studying and teaching accelerated learning techniques, life skills and peak performance strategies.

Using many of these tools, David obtained a bronze medal in the Mind Sports Olympiad, competed in the World Memory Championships, learned how to speed-read, mastered the art of mind-mapping, completed seven marathons in seven days in the gruelling Sahara Ultra-marathon across 160 miles of punishing desert terrain in Morocco and completed several fire-walks across hot coals. He has coached several world-class athletes on mind conditioning, including British long-distance swimmer and multiple world record holder Lewis Pugh, the first man ever to complete a long distance swim at the North Pole without a wetsuit.

David conducts seminars and workshops on accelerated learning, peak performance strategies and life skills training in the UK, USA and South Africa. David is the proud father of two children.

ACKNOWLEDGEMENTS

This project would not have come about without valuable assistance and advice from the following: Tim Ivison, Alison Drummond, Gina Lazar, Mark Selby, Peter Sage, Brendan Mcnutt, Tania Adams, Robbie Briggs, Rebecca Bukenya, Ed Chantler, Judy Newman, Jeff Peters, Caryl Stanley, Tracy Spilhaus, Phillipa Johnstone, Alan Kleynhans, Maxine Clancy, Brad Goz, Kyla Dixon, Osama Baldo, Kelly Deitz, Kathryn Grace, John Gibbon, Gary and Lara Blumberg, Hilary Moore, Audrey Hoonhout, Claire de la Haye, Julie Junor, Sheri Neumayer, Bryan Baguley, Jeremy Gibbon and Bridget Gibbs.

To my real-life genies, Gil Dove, Andrew Grahame, Martin Jenkins, Mark Weston, Rory Kilmartin and Brendan Mcnutt, thank you for your blessings.

Special thanks to my wife Siobhan Gallagher for your astonishing support and encouragement.

Finally, a mountain of gratitude to my own parents, Derek and Mary Becker, who have always inspired me to learn and encouraged me to teach.

'Apart from providing a valuable and inspirational teaching tool for teachers, this book will delight anyone passionate about how we should prepare the next generation for life.'

Jeff Peters, Activities Director, Antelope Union High School, Arizona, USA and Associate Director of the Arizona Association of Student Councils

'This material offers an insightful and helpful approach to tackling some of the more delicate and challenging topics that form part of the curriculum as well as preparing children and young adults for our world today.'

Camilla Howell, Deputy Headteacher and Extended Schools Coordinator, Hobbayne Primary School, London, UK

'*50 Life Skills to Ensure Kids Stay In School, Off Drugs and Out of Trouble* reminds us of that inner, healthy, natural wisdom we can share with our children. It presents us beautifully with basic tools for a fulfilling life and allows us to pass them on to our children in a fun way. It is a breath of fresh air and a delightfully valuable book!'

Gina Lazar, mother of two, aged 8 and 12

CONTENTS

INTRODUCTION

It has occurred to me on numerous occasions during the course of my life that many important life lessons and skills which are so vital for our personal growth and development are not taught in schools and universities generally.

Certainly, they were not taught to me during my school years – nor were they taught to me during my university degree or my postgraduate degree. It was, regrettably, left up to me to discover these lessons and learn these skills in a rather arbitrary and haphazard fashion, with the help of some creative parenting, a few enlightened teachers and various leaders in the field of personal development, to whom I am eternally grateful.

What I have provided in this workbook (playbook!) is a fun guide which will enable teachers, parents and caregivers to teach, or rather allow children to discover and learn, some of these important lessons and skills – lessons and skills which, if understood correctly, will have a significant influence in developing the wisdom of the child.

For it is ultimately wisdom that we seek for our children. Intelligence is a handy start, yes - although I would hasten to add that I have met many intelligent people who are not wise. It is wisdom that will enable the children of today to discern, distinguish, and evaluate. It is wisdom that will guide them to make the choices which will better serve them in their lives.

But how to develop wisdom in a child?

The answer is through understanding.

Often teachers, parents and caregivers focus on *giving* the lesson rather than ensuring *comprehension*. This is one of the reasons why children sometimes develop negative associations to learning.

What children need is to understand through realization and discovery. Anyone who has ever had an 'A-ha!' moment will know why. The lesson is not easily forgotten. As Scottish theologian William Barclay once observed:

 That which is merely told is quick to be forgotten; that which is discovered lasts a lifetime.

Leading educationalist Peter Kline, author of *The Everyday Genius* agrees:

 Children learn best when they are helped to discover the underlying principles for themselves.

The truth is that children are more likely to discover and understand when all their senses are captivated – this can be achieved by ensuring that lessons are entertaining, stimulating and engaging. For best results, lessons need to be fun. As Bob Pike, Director of Creative Training Techniques has stated:

 People learn in direct proportion to how much fun they are having.

Games not only provide entertainment and stimulation, but also allow children to participate. And it is that active participation which is the key to successful learning.

The aim of this book then is to provide a collection of fun, interactive and meaningful activities which teachers, parents and caregivers can share with children, allowing them to discover, experience and learn the life lessons and skills which will guide them as they grow older. I suspect that the facilitators may also learn a thing or two…

HOW TO USE THIS BOOK

The activities and games have been designed to facilitate understanding in a playful manner. They are very simple and do not require much time or many props. In most cases, they can be played in the classroom (as part of a PSHE, Citizenship or Character Education curriculum), in a playgroup or at home. Each activity demonstrates an important life lesson or skill.

Those for younger children (aged 6 and upwards) are located near the front of the book, with those for slightly older children contained in the sections following. Each life lesson or skill also contains a further, more advanced game or activity which is intended for slightly older children.

The specified ages should only be used as a guide. The reality is that some children are more advanced than others, or perhaps simply more receptive to learning the life lesson or skill. You are encouraged to make your own decisions based on your knowledge of the participants.

Although the masculine gender is used throughout when referring to the participants, this is only for practical purposes and the activities are suitable for both girls and boys.

Each life lesson or skill contains a toolbox for the game, suggested age, directions in preparation for the game, a description of the game itself, an explanation of the lesson or skill, the optional and more advanced game or exercise to further illustrate the lesson or skill and, finally, a summary of the life lesson or skill. There are also a number of poster pages containing quotes relating to the lessons or skills, which can be put on a wall or pinboard as a reminder.

In each case the game or activity is designed to form a basis for discussion of the relevant topic. The described game or activity is only a suggestion aimed at providing a fun platform for that discussion. Teachers, parents and caregivers are encouraged to adapt the material, or supplement it, as the circumstances require. Perhaps add a few life lessons or skills of your own that have not been included!

Please do not be shy to share your own games and activities with us. Email us using the address below and let us know of other useful games and activities that can be used to demonstrate valuable life lessons and skills. The more variety and fun we can inject into learning, the more effective we will be in enhancing the education that children will receive.

David Becker
info@davidbecker.co.uk

February 2008

50 Life skills

GAMES FOR AGES 6 AND UPWARDS

1 Tolerance

> Since the beginning of time, there have been 70 billion people
> – each one astonishingly different from all the others.
>
> Tony Buzan

Toolbox

Several apples of different colours, sizes and shapes (if possible, one for each participant).
Cutting knife.

Directions

- Select a few apples that are different in size, colour and shape.

Activity

- Hold up these apples in front of the participants, demonstrating the different colours, shapes and sizes.
- Take the knife and slice one apple in half across the apple (not lengthwise, as you would normally do).
- Ask the participants what they notice about the apple.
- Demonstrate that the apple has a perfect five-pointed star inside it that holds the seeds.
- Now cut a few of the other apples in half to show that, regardless of the colour, shape or size, they all contain the beautiful five-pointed star inside them.

Explanation

People are a lot like apples. You will come across people of all different colours, shapes, sizes and colours in life. Each person is different. Similarly, no two apples are alike. Despite all of our differences, each person, like the apple, carries within them a beautiful star. The star inside each of us represents the unique gifts that we bring to the world, e.g. love, laughter, compassion, courage etc.

The seeds represent the potential in all of us to grow and develop these gifts.

Encourage the participants to look beyond the outer qualities of colour, size, shape, beauty or age, and consider the inner gifts and value of each person with whom they interact. It is what is on the inside that counts.

Tip: using sheets of different coloured wrapping paper for the well-known game Pass the Parcel can also demonstrate this life lesson effectively.

Further Activity

- Encourage each participant to pick a partner.
- Get them to guess what special gift their partner carries deep inside them. Encourage them to use their imagination, if necessary.
- Once they have completed this, have each of the participants explain to the group what special gift they found in their partner. It could be that he or she has neat handwriting or is good at baking or kicking a soccer ball.
- Alternatively, if you can, take a trip outside where there are some trees. See if you can find several different coloured leaves growing on the same tree. Notice that they are all different, but living together harmoniously on the same tree.

Life Lesson/Skill

During your lifetime you will come across many people of a different colour, creed, size and shape. Everyone is different in some way. Learn to accept the differences in people. Remember that within their core, each person carries a special gift to share with the world.

Love everyone.
Love as one
human being to another,
who just happens to be
white or black,
rich or poor,
enemy or friend.

Vince Lombardi

2

Sticking Together

 When spider webs unite, they tie up a lion.
African proverb

Toolbox

A number of long, thin, straight sticks, about 3 cm in diameter (at least eight in number), or alternatively, a box of toothpicks.
A piece of thick rope or bounded wire (optional).

Directions

- If possible, get the participants to collect the sticks outside.

Activity

- Take one stick and hold it up.
- Then announce to the participants: 'This stick is you.'
- Once you have done this, break the stick in two.
- Now hold up all the sticks together, side by side.
- Try to break the sticks in front of the participants. You should not be able to do it.
- Announce, as you try to break the sticks together: 'This is your family.'

Explanation

When people 'stick' together, there is power. They are always able to accomplish more. They can depend on each other, and provide support for one another.

So it is with your family unit. You are the stick. Sometimes one person alone can be 'broken' – distressed, sad, overwhelmed, hurt. However, with the support of your family, each person becomes more powerful. When you are with your family you are much stronger. You will have more 'stickability'. Stick together and you will get through anything. You will be 'unbreakable'.

Tip: you might wish to turn the above activity into a story, such as: 'When I was a young child, my grandfather and I were out walking in the forest and came across a stick. My grandfather held it up and showed it to me, saying, "This is you"'…etc. Children like stories. However, if you want to ensure impact, get them to imagine that they are the stick!

This game can also be played with toothpicks if you are unable to find suitable sticks in the vicinity or there is not enough time for the children to collect the sticks.

Further Activity

- Take a piece of thick rope or bounded wire.
- Encourage the participants to gather around.
- Ensure that the end of the rope or wire is flayed slightly. The participants will see that the rope or wire consists of many thin strips placed one on top of the other.
- Encourage them to recognize that alone, each one is flimsy and weak. Together they are strong and tough.

For families who have experienced divorce, separation, or the death of a family member, it would be useful to discuss how any size family should be regarded as a family unit and can still feel a great sense of companionship and bonding when facing the world together (also, if you are aware of someone who has no family, or is in an abusive family environment, this game can be adapted to refer to a 'support group' or 'loved ones' instead).

Alone, we can easily be 'broken' and helpless. Your family unit can provide support and strength. Together you will have more 'stickability'. 'Stick' together no matter what and you will be unbreakable.

Call it a clan,
call it a network,
call it a tribe,
call it a family.

Whatever you call it,
whoever you are,
you need one.

Jane Howard

3 Honesty

 Honesty is the first chapter in the book of wisdom.
Thomas Jefferson

Toolbox

A ball of yarn or string.
A chair.
Bleach (optional).
Food colouring (optional).
Three drinking glasses (optional).

Directions

- Before you begin, arrange with one of the participants to give a false answer to each question you ask him.
- Arrange the participants so that they are sitting in a circle around the chair.

Activity

- Begin by asking everyone in the group to think of a time when they decided to tell the truth, even when it may have been easier not to do so. Ask them how it felt to tell the truth.
- Ask the designated person (your confidant) to sit in the chair.
- Begin by asking him a simple question about his day.
- As he answers with a lie, wrap a long string of 'yarn' around him, so that he is tied to the chair.
- Now ask a further question based on the first reply. As he makes up another answer, wrap the yarn around him once again.
- Continue to ask him further questions around the same incident or circumstance, each time wrapping the yarn around him as he tells a lie.
- Soon enough, he will be all tied up, entangled in a web of yarn.
- Explain to the participants that you asked the person in the chair to answer each question with a lie.
- Finally, ask the participants to observe the web in which the person has become entangled.

Explanation

This game illustrates how important it is to tell the truth. Once we begin to tell one lie, it becomes easy, and sometimes necessary, to tell another. We begin to weave a web of deceit around ourselves. Soon we become trapped in a web of lies from which we cannot escape.

A person who is always honest is truly free (he is not tied to the chair). He does not have to remember what his last lie was or how he covered up the truth. He has a clear conscience, peace of mind and feels good about himself.

Even when someone has told a lie, it is best to 'come clean' as soon as possible. By coming clean and telling the truth, he will break himself free from the entangled web instantly and be freed (as is the case when the string is cut with a pair of scissors).

Further Activity

- Fill two drinking glasses about half full of water.
- Fill the third glass about half full of bleach (household 'chlorine bleach' works best).
- Indicate to the participants that the two glasses represent two people, Mark and Geoff.
- Explain that while Mark is someone who is honest and always tells the truth, Geoff always tends to be crossing the line and getting himself into trouble. Geoff cheated on his school test, lied to his parents about his grades, stole a chocolate bar from the shop, and sprayed paint on the neighbour's wall.
- As you relate each thing that Geoff did, add one drop of food colouring to Geoff's glass each time, without stirring.
- In time, Geoff felt unhappy and lonely. Mark and his other friends no longer wished to spend time with him because he was constantly getting into hot water. He had become entangled in all his lies and dishonesty. After a long talk with his parents, he decided to change his ways.

- He admitted to the teacher that he had cheated on the test, told the truth to his parents about his grades, repaid the shop owner for the chocolate bar and helped the neighbour clean up his wall.
- For each of these actions taken by Geoff, pour about a teaspoon of bleach into his glass. The participants will think that you are merely adding more water to Geoff's glass, but they will be amazed as the coloured water starts to clear. Soon it will almost be completely clear again.
- Appropriate caution should be exercised in conducting this activity.

Each time that Geoff was dishonest, so his glass became more and more clouded, the 'stain' finally pervading his entire glass and filling him with guilt.

However, it is never too late to tell the truth and 'clear things up' again. As soon as Geoff began to tell the truth, his glass began to clear again. As a result, he became happier and felt better about himself.

Life Lesson/Skill

Always be honest. Telling a lie can lead to a tangled web of deceit from which it is hard to escape. Telling the truth literally does 'set you free' and will make you happier and more at ease with yourself.

If you tell the truth you never have to remember anything.

Mark Twain

4 Trust

It is impossible to get through life without trust
– that is to be imprisoned in the worst possible cell, oneself.
Graham Greene

Toolbox

A blindfold (optional).
Chairs, boxes, tins and other similar obstacles (optional).

Directions

- Select a participant to come forward.

Activity

- Ask the participant to stand up straight and close his eyes.
- Position yourself directly behind him and tell him that on the count of three he is going to make himself as stiff as a plank and then fall backwards, and that he has to trust that you are going to catch him. Ask the participant whether he trusts that you will catch him when he falls. If not, assure him that you will catch him until he is confident enough to conduct the activity.
- Ensuring that the participant is standing up straight, with his arms at his sides and legs straight, encourage him to fall backwards into your arms.
- Repeat the activity a few times, until the participant is falling confidently back into your arms.
- If the group is a small one, encourage each participant to have a turn, so that they can experience the feeling of trust for themselves. If the group is a large one and the participants are old enough, you can divide the group into pairs to conduct the activity. Tip: be sure to divide the participants into evenly-sized pairings for safety. If the participants are young, conduct each activity personally.

Explanation

It is an essential, and indeed healthy, part of a child's development that he learns to trust others – particularly those close to him. As people get to know one another better, they learn to trust in one another. In turn, trusting one another leads to a strengthening of the relationship. Deep, meaningful relationships are usually built on a strong foundation of trust.

We should not automatically trust those people we don't know very well (at this point you may wish to discuss with the participants when it is safe to trust someone and when it is not). However, over time and through familiarity we can usually learn to trust those who are close to us and prove trustworthy.

Ask the participant how it felt to trust their partner during the activity. Point out that in the beginning they may have had some uncertainty about the activity, but each time as they conducted the activity their trust grew with experience.

Further Activity

- In a large room or outside, gather a number of obstacles, some large and some small. Good examples are chairs, stools, plastic containers, boxes, tins and cushions.
- Place the obstacles around the room or play area so that you design an 'obstacle course'.
- Blindfold a participant and explain that he may select someone he trusts to guide him around the room so that he completes the 'obstacle course' successfully. However, that person is not permitted to guide him physically – only through verbal instruction.
- Other participants are entitled to try to lead him astray by giving him false directions as he proceeds, but he should listen only to the person he trusts.
- Note: Only select a participant who is comfortable wearing a blindfold.
- After each participant or a number of selected participants (depending on the size of the group) have completed the activity successfully, discuss with the group how it was necessary to trust their partner.

The obstacle course is a lot like life. We face challenges in our path from time to time. The distractions from the other participants are also similar to the distractions we face in everyday life. It is important to have someone you can trust to assist you as you overcome these challenges.

Life Lesson/Skill

In order for our relationships to grow and develop, we have to learn to trust people that are close to us. Once we can trust our friends, family and caregivers, we are able to rely on them as a good source of support.

The chief lesson I have learned in a long life is that the only way to make a man trustworthy is to trust him.

Henry Stimson

5 The Power of Visualization

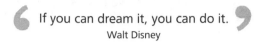

" If you can dream it, you can do it. "
Walt Disney

Toolbox

An open space indoors or outdoors.
Piece of chalk, tape or rope.

Directions

- Set a line on the floor using the chalk, tape or rope.
- Encourage all the participants to stand with their two feet together on the line. If there is not enough room, the participants should form a queue and take it in turns to play the game.

Activity

- Each participant should be encouraged to see how far he can jump from the line with his feet together.
- With the chalk or tape, mark a spot on the floor where that participant has landed.
- Now explain that you are going to weave a bit of magic!
- Have the participant close his eyes and imagine doing the jump again, except this time he jumps even further. Let the participant picture in his mind the mark where he landed, and then imagine himself sailing through the air and landing far past it, and you drawing a new mark.
- Now try the exercise again. If done correctly, the second jump will always be further.

Explanation

In this game the participants experience an increase in performance (going right past the spot) in a very short space of time through using the art of visualization.

Visualization is a fantastic tool to use when confronted by a challenge, or to increase performance in any project. Kids have a wonderful imagination and should be encouraged to use it to their benefit to prepare for an event in the future.

What is usually illustrated is an approximate 25 per cent increase in performance in about one minute. Imagine what can be done if a child spends a full five minutes imagining their successful performance before the event!

Tip: the more colourful, wacky and bizarre the image, the more the mind will capture that image and store it successfully.

Further Activity

Here is a slightly more advanced version of the same activity. Demonstrate the following:

1 Stand up and raise your right arm horizontally out in front of you, pointing with the index finger. Keeping the arm horizontal and keeping both feet in a fixed position and facing forward, turn the right arm to the right. Swivel around to the right with the right arm as far as it can go, without moving the feet.

2 When you have turned as far with your arm as you are able to, mark a spot on the wall or on the horizon in your mind.

3   Return to a forward-facing position, with hands at your side. Now close your eyes and imagine lifting your right arm horizontally and turning the arm around the furthest you are able to, but imagining this time that you are going right past the spot marked on the wall or horizon – a foot or more past the original spot.

4   Open your eyes and do the activity again with the right arm, holding it horizontal and swivelling to the right to see how far around you are able to turn with feet facing forward. You will be able to go right past the original spot by some distance.

Each participant should now do the exercise himself.

Suggest that each participant think of an upcoming challenge or event. Get them to close their eyes and relax, then see themselves in their mind performing the task successfully. Further enhance the image by getting the participant to make the picture as colourful, big and bright as possible, moving and with sound, as if they were in their own movie! Ask them to describe how it makes them feel. Do they feel happy or excited? Encourage them to allow those feelings of happiness and excitement to grow even stronger.

Encourage each participant to imagine this every day for even better results.

Tip: if the participant is having trouble trying to imagine something in his mind's eye, encourage him to close his eyes and 'paint a picture' with a big paintbrush. Encourage him to 'paint' with as many senses as possible, using colours, tastes, sounds and smells.

Life Lesson/Skill

Skill: Visualize yourself reaching your goals and overcoming your challenges and you will improve your performance with little effort!

The future
belongs
to those
who believe
in the beauty of
their dreams.

Eleanor Roosevelt

6 Self-confidence

 Life shrinks or expands in proportion to one's courage.
Anais Nin

Toolbox

Some empty cardboard boxes (such as shoe boxes or tissue boxes), cartons and plastic containers.
Markers.
Pad of paper.
Sticky labels large enough to write on.
Bandana or piece of cloth.

Directions

- Gather together the boxes, cartons and containers.
- This game can be played with a single nominated participant, with each participant in turn or in groups as part of a cooperative learning exercise.

Activity

- Encourage the participant to think of a goal he would like to achieve e.g. saving for a bike, learning to swim, sleeping without the light on, making the football team.
- Arrange for the goal to be written on a piece of paper and stuck up on the wall or on a board.
- Now discuss the things that are preventing the participant from attaining that goal e.g. temptation to spend money on junk, fear, monsters in the hallway, lack of self-confidence.
- Explain that these things are all obstacles which are preventing him from moving forward and attaining that goal. They are like a wall between him and the goal.
- Write these obstacles on labels or stickers and attach them to the various boxes.
- Now encourage the participant to stack up the boxes so that they physically form a wall between him and the goal.
- Discuss what special skills and attributes the participant has to help him overcome these stumbling blocks, such as courage, having creativity or being a good organizer.
- As you talk, write each of those qualities on a sticker and attach it to the participant.
- Suggest that with these special skills and attributes, he can break through the barriers which face him and accomplish the goal (and any other goal, for that matter).
- Now the really fun part! Encourage the participant to tie a bandana around his head and recite an unusual chant or an empowering incantation ('All I need is within me now!'). Encourage him to imagine what it will feel like once he has broken through the barriers. Tell him to turn and face the wall. Finally, encourage him to recite his chant or incantation and demolish the wall entirely with several short, sharp karate kicks (this may sound violent, but kids love this game and it can be used as a supporting reference many times later on in their lives).

Explanation

When setting and reaching for our goals, the thing which most prevents us from attaining them is lack of confidence, or fear. People can go through their entire lives not doing the things they really want to do because they build up a wall of fear. As they focus on the wall of fear in front of them, it tends to get bigger and bigger, until they can no longer see the goal on the other side.

It is helpful in these circumstances to focus instead on the skills and resources we have that will help us break down the barriers and overcome the obstacles. We all have special skills and resources at our disposal. More importantly, when we use them, they tend to grow.

Another way to change focus when constrained by fear is to ask the question: '*What would you do if you weren't afraid?*'

You may find this acronym useful:

FEAR   =   False
           Expectations
           Appearing
           Real

Further Activity

The activity below is a very simple but effective one in building problem-solving and decision-making skills, which in turn help to develop self-confidence. It can be played anywhere at any time.

- Ask the participants a series of questions, beginning each with the words: '*What would you do if…?*'
- After each answer, encourage discussion of the proposed scenario and follow up with further questions, such as: '*What if that didn't work?*' and '*What else could you do?*'
- The kind of question can vary in importance and theme. Here are some examples:

What would you do if…
  o You were at a shopping centre and you were lost and could not find your mother or father anywhere?
  o A man who you do not know arrives at school to pick you up, saying that your mother had asked him to pick you up because her car had broken down?
  o Your friend asks you for the questions to a school test you had taken earlier?
  o You were riding home from school on your bike and fell off and you were bleeding?
  o While playing with a ball you accidentally hit it against a nearby car and it dented the bonnet?
  o The person who is supposed to give you a ride home fails to show up?
  o You are locked out of your house and there is no one inside?
  o You are sleeping at a friend's house and you get scared because of the strange surroundings?
  o The older brother of a friend offers to give you a ride home and you think they have had too much to drink?
  o A friend invited you over to play and then shortly afterwards another friend calls and asks you to come over swimming the same afternoon?
  o You accidentally lost your lunch money?
  o You lend one of your friends a toy and he breaks it?
  o Someone keeps teasing you and calling you names at school?

Vary the questions according to the age of the participants. If you are concerned about a particular response, discuss it further. Discussing the various options available to a participant helps them manage any fears they might have, prevents unnecessary worrying and helps them act appropriately and with confidence if the circumstances arise. The aim is not to focus on the fear itself, but on an empowering response to it.

Life Lesson/Skill

The barrier which most prevents us from achieving our goals is fear. When facing your fears, focus on the skills and attributes that you have inside of you, not on the fear itself, and you will find the courage and confidence to break through the barrier.

Obstacles
are those
frightful things
you see when you take
your eyes off your goal.

Henry Ford

7 **Priorities**

 Don't major in minor things.
Anon

Toolbox

One large empty glass or clear plastic jar.
Approximately six or seven small rocks or large stones, as required.
Approximately three handfuls of pebbles, as required.
Approximately four handfuls of sand, as required.
Pack of cards (optional).

Directions

- Display the jar and the rocks on a table in front of the participants.
- Hide the pebbles and sand for the moment.

Activity

- Pick up the jar and fill it with the rocks.
- Ask the participants if they believe that the jar is full (the reply sought is 'Yes'!)
- Pick up the pebbles and now pour the pebbles into the jar.
- Shake the jar slightly so that the pebbles roll into the open areas between the rocks.
- Ask the participants if they believe that the jar is now full (again, the reply sought is 'Yes').
- Now take out the sand and pour it into the jar. The sand should fill up everything else.

Explanation

The jar represents your life. The rocks are the important things, such as your family (or loved ones), your education or your health – things with which if everything else was lost and only they remained, your life would still be full.

The pebbles are the other things that matter like your friends, your home and your bicycle.

The sand is everything else. It's the small stuff, like your toys, for instance.

If you put the sand into the jar first, there will be no room for the rocks or the pebbles. The same goes for life. If you spend all your time and energy on the small stuff, you will never have room for the things that are really important – such as your family, your education and your health.

Pay attention to the rocks in your life – those are the things that are essential to your happiness. Spend time with your family. Take care of your body. Read an interesting book. Learn something new. There will always be time for the small stuff. Take care of the rocks first, and then the pebbles. Set your priorities. The rest is just sand.

Tip: the larger the jar and the more colourful the rocks and pebbles, the more you will be able to hold the attention of the participants.

Further Activity

- Is the jar now really full…? What else might you be able to fit in the jar?
- Encourage the participants to think of some possibilities. Usually they will come up with some creative answers!
- Encourage the participants to see if they can build a house with a pack of cards. This could entertain them for hours! They will soon realize that without a solid foundation, the house of cards will not last very long. It is important to get the foundations right first, and build from there.

Take care of the rocks in your life first. These are the important things. Then the pebbles. Then the sand. Learn to prioritize the important things in life first.

The winds blew and beat upon that house; and it fell not:

for it was founded upon a rock.

Bible – Matthew 7.25

8 Be the Light

 In helping others, we shall help ourselves, for whatever good
we give out completes the circle and comes back to us.
Flora Edwards

Toolbox

A box or boxes of candles, as required (at least two candles).
A box of matches.
Pieces of A3- or A4-sized paper (optional).
Pencils/pens as required (optional).
Scissors (optional).

Directions

- Get the participants to stand or sit in a circle, each holding a candle. Now dim the lights.

Activity

- Hold and light one of the candles.
- Pass on the flame to one of the participants by lighting his candle. Instruct the participant to pass on the flame in turn by lighting his neighbour's candle with his own candle.
- When he passes the flame on, get him to say 'I now pass on my light to you.'
- Continue with this until each participant's candle is lit.

Explanation

A candle loses nothing by lighting another candle.

You might think that when you give of yourself to others, that which is inside you diminishes or becomes less. That is not true.

In life, when you give love, joy, warmth and happiness to others, the love, joy, warmth and happiness inside you will not diminish. Like the candle flame, you lose nothing by giving it away. In fact, you gain, because it increases inside of you.

When you give of your light to others, the light inside you grows. Also, the people who have received the light from you can pass it on to others, and so the light is shared and passed out into the world.

Tip: make sure that you don't do this activity near any flammable objects.

Further Activity

- Stop by at a nearby church or temple. One can usually find candles for lighting inside. Encourage the children to light a candle for the people that they love and say a prayer. Notice that as the flame spreads, so does the love.
- Alternatively, play the picture multiplication game. Hand out a piece of A4- or A3-sized paper to each participant. Holding each piece of paper horizontally, each participant should fold over the paper about the width of a ruler, and then make subsequent folds, one on top of the other until they run out of paper. On the front strip, encourage them to draw a picture of a heart with a pencil or pen, so that the sides of the heart touch the left and right hand side of the strip.
- Have the participants cut out the heart. When the paper is unfolded a multitude of hearts should be displayed, each one magically connected to the other.

Life Lesson/Skill

A candle loses nothing by lighting another candle. As the flame passes from one candle to another, it does not diminish – it multiplies. Give freely of your love, joy, warmth and happiness to others and so it will multiply and increase in you.

I am of the opinion that my life
belongs to the whole community
and as long as I live,
it is my privilege to do for it
whatever I can.
I want to be fully used up when I die,
for the harder I work, the more I love.
I rejoice in life for its own sake.
Life is no brief candle for me.
It is a sort of splendid torch
which I have got to hold
for the moment
and I want to make it burn
as brightly as possible
before handing it on
to future generations.

George Bernard Shaw

9 Goal Setting

 The indispensable first step to getting the things you want out of life is this: decide what you want.

Ben Stein

Toolbox

Large piece of paper or poster (preferably A3 or larger).
One pencil.
One eraser.
Pair of scissors.
Blu-tack or another adhesive putty or roll of sticking tape. (These are preferred to a thumbtack or drawing pin for safety reasons).
One blindfold (any dark piece of cloth should do).
Bow and arrow set (optional). (Obtainable from most toy stores.)
Paper and pens/pencils as required (optional).

Directions

- Pin the poster up against a cupboard or wall.
- With the pencil draw a large donkey in the middle of the paper. Remember *not* to draw the tail!
- Cut a small strip of paper from the side of the paper (curly if you can!) and, on one end, make a few small parallel cuts to make frays. Alternatively, use an old piece of material or strip of wool. This will be the tail of the donkey.
- Attach the Blu-tack or putty or a piece of sticky tape to the top of the tail.

Activity

- Each participant should apply the blindfold and take it in turns to try and pin the tail on the donkey in the correct place.
- Once a participant has pinned the tail in a particular spot, mark the spot with the initials of the participant.

Tip: turning the person around once or twice will make it a bit more challenging!

Explanation

It is important to have a target in life to know where you are heading. Otherwise you may walk through life quite aimlessly, and may never get to fulfil the unique potential that lies within you.

Here's the key to remember: *It is hard to hit a target when you don't know where it is*. Kids should have targets for themselves, otherwise known as goals. These targets should be specific, described clearly and identified with precision. Also, kids must know when they have hit the target!

Kids often ask: how big should my goals be? A good place to start is with the premise that goals should be just out of reach, but not out of sight. Once kids have set and reached a few short-term goals and gathered confidence in the process of setting and achieving goals, they should be encouraged to set bigger and more challenging goals.

Further Activity

- Another great extension of the above activity is to use a plastic bow and arrow. Set up a board with a target on it. Blindfold each participant and get each of them to try to hit the target without being able to see it.
- Read the story The Jar of Fleas on page 21. Consider and discuss how limiting beliefs can prevent us from setting and reaching our goals.
- After the activity, have each participant write down or identify three goals for the next year. You might encourage them to think of something they wish to be better in, something they wish to achieve, or

something they wish to learn. Help each participant describe the goals clearly and the date by which they will have attained the goals. Establish the reasons why they have chosen those goals (this helps to crystallize their motivation and build desire). How will they know when they have hit the target? What action steps will they need to take to hit the target?

In order to facilitate the above process, have the participants lie down and close their eyes. Now get them to imagine that they have just awoken from a one-year sleep…

Encourage the participants to describe how it feels to have achieved the goals. What does it mean to them to have achieved the goals? What have they learned in achieving the goals?

Life Lesson/Skill

It is hard to hit a target when you don't know where it is – set targets you can see or imagine clearly, make them specific and plan the steps you need to take to hit the target.

The Jar of Fleas

Max Murphy wanted to train some fleas for his new flea circus, so he found some dogs and cats and soon caught about ten strong, high-jumping fleas. Max wanted fleas that were healthy and strong, so the higher they jumped, the better. But you can't train a flea who can jump clear across a room without first getting its attention.

So high jumping was the first habit of Max's new fleas that he had to break.

At first, the fleas were in a big cage where they had plenty of jumping room. So Max transferred them one by one to a jar about five inches high. After that, each time a flea jumped, he banged his whole body on the lid of the jar. Obviously, continual body banging felt very uncomfortable to the fleas. As a result, they began to jump with less vigour, so that when they banged themselves it wouldn't hurt as much (but it still hurt).

After a while, they jumped with even less vigour, until finally one flea made a very weak jump and went down again without banging himself at all! As soon as the other fleas saw this, they copied him, and pretty soon all of the fleas were jumping up and down inside the jar without hitting the lid.

Max had been watching carefully, but he didn't take the lid off – yet. He wanted the fleas to get so used to having the lid there, and jumping little jumps, that they wouldn't miss the lid after it was gone. They would not even remember how to make big jumps.

And that's exactly what happened. After several more days, Max took off the lid and, sure enough, there were those poor little fleas jumping up and down, but never higher than four-and-three-quarter inches…for the rest of their lives.

10 Challenges

' When we look deeply into the heart of a flower, we see clouds, sunshine, minerals, time, the earth and everything else in the cosmos in it. Without clouds, there could be no rain, and without rain there would be no flower. '

Thich Nhat Hanh

Toolbox

One carrot.
One egg.
Some coffee beans or hot chocolate powder.
Three pots and a stove or cooker.
One rose (optional).

Directions

- You may choose to read out the story below, or actually conduct the activity, depending on the circumstances.
- Conducting the activity will leave a greater impression; however it may not be possible to get access to a portable stove or cooker.

Activity

- The story is set out below:

A daughter complained to her father about her life and how things were so hard for her. She did not know how she was going to make it and wanted to give up. She was tired of fighting and struggling. It seemed as one problem was solved a new one arose.

Her father took her into the kitchen. He filled three pots with water and placed each on a high fire. Soon the pots came to the boil. In one he placed the carrot, in the second he placed the egg, and in the last he placed ground coffee beans. He let them sit and boil, without saying a word.

The daughter sucked her teeth and impatiently waited, wondering what he was doing.

In about ten minutes he turned off the stove. He fished the carrot out and placed it in a bowl. He pulled the egg out and placed it in a bowl also. Then he ladled the coffee out and placed it in a bowl as well.

Turning to her he asked, 'Darling, what do you see?'

'A carrot, an egg and coffee,' she replied.

He brought her closer and asked her to feel the carrot.

She did and noticed that it was soft. He then asked her to take the egg and break it. After pulling off the shell, she observed the hard-boiled egg.

Finally, he asked her to sip the coffee. She smiled as she tasted its rich aroma.

She then asked, 'What does it mean father?'

He explained that each of them had faced the same adversity, boiling water, but each had reacted differently. The carrot went in strong, hard and unrelenting. But after being subjected to the boiling water, it softened and became weak.

The egg had been fragile. Its thin outer shell had protected its liquid inside. But after sitting through the boiling water, its inside became hardened.

The ground coffee beans were unique, however. After they were in the boiling water for a while, they changed the water.

'Which are you?' he asked his daughter. 'When adversity or hardship comes knocking on your door, how do you respond? Are you a carrot, an egg, or a coffee bean?'

Are you the carrot that seems hard, but with hardship and adversity you wilt and become soft and lose your strength?

Are you the egg, which starts off with a soft heart? Were you a fluid spirit, but after facing a challenge have you become hardened and stiff? Your shell looks the same, but are you bitter and tough with a stiff spirit and heart?

Or are you like the coffee bean? The bean changes the hot water, the thing that is bringing the pain, and allows it to develop into something pleasurable. When the water gets the hottest, it just tastes better.

How do you handle a challenge?
Are you like the carrot or the egg? Or are you like the coffee bean – when things are at their worst, you get better and make things better around you?

Tip: If you want to conduct the activity yourself, which is recommended, you can speed it up by putting the pots on the boil a few minutes before you begin the activity.

Further Activity

- Hold the rose up in front of the participants.
- Have each participant examine the rose carefully. Allow them to lightly run their fingers up the stem, feeling the prickly thorns, the rough base of the stem, the soft petals and the delicate filaments which make up the stamen.

A rose is very much like life: you will meet thorns (challenges) along the way, but if you have faith, courage and determination you will eventually move beyond the thorns and experience the magnificence of the flower.

When faced with a challenge, participants should be encouraged to try to come up with a solution where everyone wins (called a 'win-win' solution). See Chapter 44 for a more direct illustration of this skill.

Finally, or as an alternative, read the Parable of the Mule below.

Life Lesson/Skill

From time to time, you will face challenges in your life. How you respond will display your character. Are you a carrot or an egg? Or are you like the coffee bean: when the heat is on, you get better and make things better around you?

The Parable of the Mule

There once was a farmer who owned a mule. One day the mule fell into the farmer's well and the farmer heard the mule braying. After carefully assessing the situation, the farmer sympathized with the mule, but decided it wasn't worth saving either the mule or the well. As a result, he called his neighbours together, told them what happened, and asked them to help haul dirt to bury the old mule in the well and put him out of his misery.

At first the mule was hysterical, but as the farmer and his neighbours continued shovelling and the dirt hit his back, a thought struck him. It occurred to him that every time a shovel load of dirt landed on his back, he could shake it off and step up. And so he did! Blow after blow he repeated to himself, 'Shake it off and step up…shake it off and step up…shake it off and step up.'

No matter how painful the blows or how distressing the situation seemed, the old mule fought panic and just kept right on shaking it off and stepping up. It wasn't long before the old mule, battered and exhausted, stepped triumphantly over the wall of the well. What seemed as if it would bury him actually helped him just because of the way he handled his adversity.

The ultimate measure
of a man is not
where he stands
in moments of
comfort and convenience,
but where he stands in
times of challenge and
controversy.

Martin Luther King, Jr.

11

Miracles

If you want to see miracles, <u>be</u> the miracle…
God, played by Morgan Freeman, in the film *Bruce Almighty*.

Toolbox

Some seeds and a planting tray (optional). (Seeds for sprouting are recommended and are obtainable in most health stores).
Mirror (optional).

Directions

- Arrange for the participants to sit in a circle – it's story time!

Activity

- Read the following inspirational story about miracles…

Only very costly surgery could save him now and it was looking like there was no one to loan them the money. She heard daddy say to her tearful mother with whispered desperation, 'Only a miracle can save him now.'

Tess went to her bedroom and pulled a glass jelly jar from its hiding place in the closet. She poured all the change out on the floor and counted it carefully.

Three times, even. The total had to be exactly perfect. No chance here for mistakes. Carefully placing the coins back in the jar and twisting the cap, she slipped out the back door and made her way six blocks to Rexall's Pharmacy with the big red Indian Chief sign above the door.

She waited patiently for the pharmacist to give her some attention but he was too busy at this moment. Tess twisted her feet to make a scuffling noise.

Nothing.

She cleared her throat with the most disgusting sound she could muster. No good. Finally she took a quarter from her jar and banged it on the glass counter. That did it!

'And what do you want?' the pharmacist asked in an annoyed tone of voice. 'I'm talking to my brother from Chicago whom I haven't seen in ages,' he said, without waiting for a reply to his question.

'Well, I want to talk to you about my brother,' Tess answered back in the same annoyed tone. 'He's really, really sick…and I want to buy a miracle.'

'I beg your pardon?' said the pharmacist.

'His name is Andrew and he has something bad growing inside his head and my daddy says only a miracle can save him now. So how much does a miracle cost?'

'We don't sell miracles here, little girl. I'm sorry but I can't help you,' the pharmacist said, softening a little. 'Listen, I have the money to pay for it. If it isn't enough, I will get the rest. Just tell me how much it costs,' said Tess.

The pharmacist's brother was a well-dressed man. He stooped down and asked the little girl, 'What kind of miracle does your brother need?'

'I don't know,' Tess replied with her eyes welling up.

'I just know he's really sick and mommy says he needs an operation. But my daddy can't pay for it, so I want to use my money.'

'How much do you have?' asked the man from Chicago.

'One dollar and eleven cents,' Tess answered barely audibly. 'And it's all the money I have, but I can get some more if I need to.'

'Well, what a coincidence,' smiled the man. 'A dollar and eleven cents is the exact price for a miracle for little brothers.' He took her money in one hand and with the other hand he grasped her mitten and said, 'Take me to where you live. I want to see your brother and meet your parents.

Let's see if I have the kind of miracle you need.'

That well-dressed man was Dr Carlton Armstrong, a surgeon, specializing in neurosurgery. The operation was completed without charge and it wasn't long until Andrew was home again and doing well. Mom and dad were happily talking about the chain of events that had led them to this place. 'That surgery,' her mother whispered, 'was a real miracle. I wonder how much it would have cost?'

Tess smiled. She knew exactly how much a miracle cost…one dollar and eleven cents…plus the faith of a little child.

Explanation

There are miracles happening all around us in everyday life. You just have to open your eyes and see them. They are everywhere. This true story is one such illustration.

And miracles don't cost anything either – not even 'one dollar and eleven cents'. They are free to those who believe.

Have faith in the power of miracles and you will get to see some in your lifetime.

Further Activity

If you want to see something miraculous, look at nature. Nature produces the most splendid, magical miracles, doesn't it?

- Encourage the participants to take a walk outside where there are some flowers.
- Ask them to stop and take a look at one flower that grabs their attention.
- Encourage them to study the slender stem, the buds, the petals, and the lines on the leaves.
- Encourage the participants to dwell, just for a minute, on mankind's incredible achievements in technology. Now remind them that even with all these amazing achievements, man can still not produce even one blade of grass or flower!
- As a project, plant a few seeds in a small pot. Water it and place it in the sun. Allow the participants the opportunity to experience the miracle of the birth of new life.

    Tip: if you have a sprouter and can sprout seeds (such as mung beans, cress or alfalfa), you will have results in just a day or two.

Consider also the miracle of the human body:

- Have the participants divide into pairs and listen to each other's heartbeats (if appropriate) or take each other's pulse. Consider that the human heart beats on average 36,000,000 times per year, pumping an equivalent of 600,000 gallons of blood through 60,000 miles of arteries, veins and capillaries.
- Get the participants to close their eyes and run their hands down their arms and legs, feeling the bones and muscles. Consider that, in order to effect body movement and environmental awareness, we have 200 finely sculptured bones, 500 intricately coordinated muscles, and seven miles of nerve fibres.
- If there is a mirror handy, encourage the participants to examine their eyes in the mirror. Consider that each human eye contains 130 million light receptors, each of which can absorb five photons (bundles of light energy) per second.
- Encourage them to hold out their ears! Consider that the human ear contains 24,000 fibres that can detect tremendous ranges as well as subtle distinctions in the molecular vibrations of the air.
- Think of the number 2,000,000. Consider that two million blood cells die every second. These are replaced immediately by two million more!
- Encourage the participants to rub their skin gently with a fingernail until they see some dry skin flakes. Consider that every cell in the human body is replaced every three months.

Finally, discuss the quotation at the top of this chapter. How might each participant *be* a miracle in someone else's life right now?

Life Lesson/Skill

There are miracles all around us. Know that miracles exist and if you believe and are observant you will get to experience them in your life.

Where there
is great love
there are always
miracles
to be found.

Willa Cather

12 Teamwork

 People have been known to achieve more working with others than against them.

Dr Allan Fromme

Toolbox

Two rolls of string.
A pair of scissors.
A box of thick elastic bands (optional).
A number of empty soft drink cans (optional).

Directions

- Divide the participants up into two even groups (if there are an odd number of participants get the extra participant to help you judge).
- Each group has to choose a leader.
- Cut the roll of string into two equal strands a few metres long.

Activity

- Each leader holds the end of a piece of string.
- The leader holds onto the string and ensures that it is threaded up through each piece of his clothing and out the other side.
- The string must then be threaded beneath the clothing of each person in the team – the team with the shortest string at the end wins.
- Once the string has been threaded through each participant's clothing, the last person clasps the other end of the string in his hand. Participants should stand as close together as possible to shorten the string!
- The judge then cuts the string at that point, so that each piece of string can be measured before announcing the winner.

Explanation

Working in a team can be fun and exhilarating. Working together, people will always accomplish more. Often a team will produce far greater results than the total of each contribution. This is known as *synergy*. This is often the case in sports in particular, when a team may have weaker individuals than its competitor, but works together in a cohesive fashion to produce a group effort that is greater than its competitor.

Working together as a team is also a very bonding experience (literally in this case!) and a great way to improve relationships.

In the above activity, participants should be encouraged to work together creatively to produce the best result.

If possible, photocopy the design on page 30 and hand each participant a copy. Have the participants cut out the design and hold it up when they are finished. Alternatively, cut out the design and hold it up in front of the participants.

Illustrate that if you hold the design in one way, it reads 'ME'. However, if you turn it over, it reads 'WE'. Use this simple activity as a means to discussing the difference between selfishness and working together.

Further Activity

- Cut the string into several pieces, each about a metre/yard in length, so that each participant has a piece of string.
- Tie the pieces of string onto an elastic band at equal junctures along the band, so that when pulled, the band forms a pointed star. There should be no more than six pieces of string tied onto a single elastic band. If there are more than six participants, they should tie their pieces onto a separate elastic band, and so on.
- The object of the game is to pull the elastic band over the soft drink can and pick up the can, placing it on a nearby table.

- To do this, the participants will have to work together to pull their pieces of string simultaneously and extend the band over the can, lifting it up onto the table before easing the band off the can again.
- This activity can be made more difficult by lengthening each string, using full cans, or requiring the participants to race against one another in teams to build a pyramid of cans! This will depend on the age and number of the participants.

Tip: this activity works best using small, thick elastic bands rather than the large, thin ones.

Finally, or as an alternative, read the story Flying in 'V' Formation below.

Life Lesson/Skill

Be a team player. Working as part of an effective team is fun and energizing and will produce far greater results than the individual efforts of many.

Flying in 'V' Formation

If you are able to watch a flock of geese flying, you will see that they fly in a 'V' formation. It has been learned that as each bird flaps its wings, it creates uplift for the bird immediately following. By flying in a 'V' formation, the whole flock adds at least another 70 per cent to its flying range than if each bird flew on its own.

People who are part of a team and share a common direction get where they are going quicker and easier, because they are travelling with the cooperation of one another and lift each other up along the way.

Whenever a goose falls out of formation it suddenly feels the drag and resistance of trying to go through it alone and quickly gets back into formation to take advantage of the power of the flock. If we have as much sense as a goose, we will stay in formation and share information with those who are headed the same way that we are going.

When the lead goose tires, he rotates back in the wing and another goose takes over. It pays to share leadership and take turns doing hard jobs.

The geese honk from behind to encourage those up front to keep their speed. Words of support and inspiration help energize those on the front line, helping them to keep pace in spite of the day-to-day pressure and fatigue. It is important that our honking be encouraging. Otherwise it's just honking!

Finally when a goose gets sick or is wounded or shot down, two geese fall out of the formation and follow the injured one down to help and protect him. They stay with him until he is either able to fly or until he is dead, and then they launch out with another formation to catch up with their group.

When one of us is down, it's up to the others to stand by us in our time of trouble. If we have the sense of a goose, we will stand by each other when things get tough. We will stay in formation with those headed where we want to go.

The next time you see a formation of geese, remember: it is a reward, a challenge and a privilege to be a contributing member of a TEAM.

The Power of Team

Together
Everyone
Achieves
More

13 Gratitude

 One single grateful thought raised to heaven is the most perfect prayer.
G.E. Lessing

Toolbox

Pad of paper and pens/pencils as required.
Envelopes (optional).
Stamps (optional).

Directions

- Hand a piece of paper and pen/pencil to each participant.

Activity

- Encourage the participants to think of someone in their lives that they need to thank – or just someone they really value but perhaps have not acknowledged in a while.
- Get each participant to write a handwritten letter to that person, thanking them for all the things that he or she has done for them in their life, and letting that person know that he or she is really valued. The letter need not be long.
- Then get them to put the letter in an envelope right there and put a stamp on it, ready for posting.
- Now encourage each participant to think of all the things that he is grateful for in his life. Suggest a few simple things.
- Finally, get the participants to sit in a circle and pick a partner. Encourage each participant to express to the group something they appreciate in their partner. (Back at home, a similar activity can also be carried out as a form of a prayer before bed. The child should be encouraged to be thankful for all the wonderful magic moments they have experienced throughout the day. Encourage them to also consider the people for whom they are grateful and to finish off with the phrase 'I appreciate you [insert name], I thank you [insert name], I love you [insert name]').

Explanation

It is important to acknowledge the blessings you have in your life. For acknowledgement is the doorway to gratitude. And gratitude is one of the most valuable of all traits, not only because it grounds you and brings you into the moment of now, in which you appreciate and celebrate fully the richness in your life, but also because it allows you to draw even more abundance into your life.

The purpose of this activity is to allow the participants to *experience* the feeling of gratitude when conducting the activity.

Furthermore, expressing gratitude to others who have helped, supported and loved you on your journey is also a way of recognizing and honouring those people. It is an important way to enrich your relationships. People like to feel valued for the help, support and love that they give. Often, we forget to thank those sincerely who have assisted us on the journey of life.

Further Activity

- If possible, arrange for photocopies to be made of page 32.
- Hand one out to each of the participants. Alternatively, read out each of the questions in turn.
- Encourage the participants to add a positive reason for each statement, starting with the word *because*.
- At the end of the exercise, encourage the participants to share their answers.

The purpose of this activity is to encourage the participants to be grateful even for the small, mundane things in everyday life. Often we tend to take it for granted that we have a roof over our head, a comfortable bed to sleep in, and food on the table. Stop and consider what your life would be like without these important blessings.

Life Lesson/Skill

Develop an attitude of gratitude. Be thankful for the many blessings that you have in your life. Acknowledge those who have helped and supported you. People like to feel valued for the help, support and love that they give.

I am grateful for my alarm clock that goes off early in the morning because… *I know I am alive.*

I am grateful for the drinking water in my home because… *over 1 billion people in the world do not have access to safe drinking water.*

I am grateful for the homework I have to do every day because…*it means that I am getting an education.*

I am grateful for the chores I am required to do at home every day because…

_____

_____

I am grateful that I have to help with dinner because…

_____

_____

I am grateful for aching and tired muscles at the end of the day because…

_____

_____

I am grateful that I have to sweep up the leaves/snow in the driveway because…

_____

_____

I am grateful for having to visit the cousins because…

_____

_____

I am grateful for …

14 Judgement

How little do they see what really is, who frame their hasty judgement upon that which seems.
Robert Southey

Toolbox

Small mirror (optional).
A note of currency e.g. a dollar or pound note (optional).

Directions

- Hold up the picture on page 34.

Activity

- Get the participants to sit in a circle.
- Hand each participant a photocopy of the picture or give each participant the opportunity to study the picture.
- Ask them if they can all see a picture of an old witch/hag.
- Point out the features of the hag.
- Now ask them if they can all see a picture of a beautiful woman. They may struggle to see this, having just seen the hag. However, with some time, each participant should now see that the picture is in fact a picture of a beautiful woman.

Explanation

A valuable lesson to learn in life is that things are often not what they seem.

There are plenty of examples. Wanderers in the desert on a hot day will see a mirage, for instance. It will appear that there is a lake of water on the horizon. But it is not real. It only appears so.

Often what appears to be an adversity can be a blessing. Often what appears to be something ugly is in fact something beautiful. Our perception plays tricks on us sometimes…

Further Activity

- Try to encourage the participants to think of other examples where our perception plays tricks on us. How about a mirror? Hold up the mirror. When you look in the mirror, things appear back to front, don't they? It presents a distorted picture of reality, which can be confusing!
- Ask for a volunteer. Ask him to put his feet together.
- Now place the note of currency on the floor lengthways in front of the participant's feet. Ask him if he thinks he will be able to jump over the note while holding on to his toes.
- Now have the participant reach down and grab onto his toes and attempt to jump over the note. He will find it almost impossible to do!

This fun game looks so easy participants will have a hard time believing that they cannot do it. If there is time, give each participant a couple of turns!

Life Lesson/Skill

It is useful to remember that often life is not what it seems. Don't be quick to judge people or circumstances. What might seem to be an old hag might actually be a beautiful woman.

15 Expressing Feelings

 By starving emotions, we become humourless, rigid and stereotyped; encouraged, they perfume life; discouraged, they poison it.
Joseph Collins

Toolbox

Two balloons (or a packet of balloons if possible).
Paper and coloured pens/pencils as required (optional).
A paper bag for each participant (optional).

Directions

- See below.
- If the participants are considered old enough, this activity can be carried out by the participants themselves, either by one of the participants in front of the group or by each participant in the group.

Activity

- Take one balloon and blow it up yourself.
- When the balloon is half filled with air, stop and hold it closed with your fingers. Explain to the participants that, along with all the good feelings we experience, such as happiness, joy and excitement, from time to time we will experience negative feelings, such as unhappiness, frustration, grief, anxiety, fear or guilt.
- Continue with the blowing up of the balloon. Once the balloon is almost fully blown, stop and hold it closed with your fingers. Explain that if we do not express these feelings, by talking about them, or writing about them or sharing them with others, they will build up inside us (now blow up the balloon further).
- If we continue to keep our feelings hidden inside us, and allow them to build up and grow, it may all become too much for us. It is almost as if we burst like the balloon (now pop the balloon or let it burst naturally) and the feelings suddenly pour out of us in unsafe or unhealthy ways, such as anger, aggression, bullying, drug abuse and depression (or we can become sick with worry or simply develop a stomach ache).
- Now blow up the second balloon until it is approximately half full. Stop and hold the balloon closed at this point.
- Explain that if we express these feelings, through speaking about them, or writing about them, or sharing them with someone we trust, it helps us to let them out and deal with them (let the air out of the balloon and note that the air passes out harmlessly).

Explanation

We all have feelings. If we keep these feelings hidden, particularly the negative ones, we allow them to build up inside us. If they keep growing and overwhelm us, we may explode like the balloon and express these feelings in an unsafe or unhealthy way, as described above.

Encourage the participants to write about their feelings in a private journal, or speak about the feelings to people they trust, such as a guidance counsellor, parent, teacher, sibling or friend.

Further Activity

- Strip the paper into pieces so that each participant has five pieces of paper. Provide each participant with a pen or pencil.
- As mentioned above, sometimes we have feelings which we keep hidden inside ourselves, just as we could hide something inside a paper bag and not let anyone see what's inside.
- Ask the participants to think of a time when they might have done this and to write down that occasion and that feeling on a strip of paper and put it in the bag.
- Ask the participants if there are feelings which they readily share with others (these are usually happy feelings). Suggest that they write down some of these feelings on the outside of their bags with coloured pens/pencils.

- Note: if the participants are very young, assist by making the annotations on the strips and bags yourself.
- Encourage the participants to share examples of feelings that they tend to keep inside, away from others, and examples of feelings they tend to share.

Tip: if the participants are of a younger age, you might suggest some of these feelings or write them down on a piece of paper.

Life Lesson/Skill

We all have many feelings. Expressing feelings is important and natural. Do not keep your feelings hidden and bottled up. Write them down or share them with others whom you trust.

Grant me some wild expressions, Heavens, or I shall burst!

George Farguhar

16   Listening

 It is the province of knowledge to speak and it is the privilege of wisdom to listen.

Oliver Wendell Holmes

Toolbox

Blindfold(s) (optional).
Sticky labels or name tags (one for each participant).
Pen.

Directions

- Divide the participants into pairs.
- Give one participant in each pair a blindfold or ask him to close his eyes or turn his back.

Activity

- Have one participant move around the room knocking on, manipulating or rubbing different things. The other party with his eyes covered should try to guess what is being knocked on, used or rubbed.
- Encourage use of different body sounds as well e.g. hand slapping the knee, feet stomping on the ground, fingers snapping, tongues clicking, mouth blowing etc.
- Allow the participants to take turns being the listener and the noise maker.

Tip: a younger participant can be asked to identify a more common sound while an older participant can be asked to identify a more subtle sound.

Explanation

To succeed in this game, you need to listen well. It is the same in life. It pays to be a good listener.

All too often in life, when we are in conversation, we are tempted to focus on what we are about to say next, rather than on what the other person is saying! Then we miss the point they are trying to make and we appear disinterested.

Being a good listener is an important attribute. It will enable you to make many friends. People value friends who can really listen to them when they are confronted with a problem or are just going through a hard time. In addition, being a good listener helps us communicate better with others.

Finally, when we listen, we tend to learn.

Further Activity

- Write random double-digit numbers in large writing on each label.
- Stick a label on the chest of each participant.
- Get the participants to sit in a circle facing inwards.
- Get one participant to start the game by saying his number.
- After the participant says his number, everyone claps twice in unison.
- The same participant then says a second person's number and again everyone claps twice in unison.
- The second participant repeats the process, saying his own number, clapping twice and saying a third number, and so on e.g. '22 clap clap, 31 clap clap; 31 clap clap, 46 clap clap; 46 clap clap, 24 clap clap'.

Life Lesson/Skill

It is important in life to be a good listener. When you listen, you learn. You will begin to hear things that other people don't hear, and will become a better communicator.

A good listener
is not only
popular everywhere,
but after a while
he gets to
know something.

Wilson Mizner

17 Happiness

> Success in its highest and noblest form comes from peace of mind and enjoyment and happiness, which comes only to the man who has found the work he likes best.
>
> Napolean Hill

Toolbox

Pad of paper and pens/pencils as required (optional).

Directions

- Hand out a pen/pencil and piece of paper to each participant.

Activity

- Encourage the participants to write down or describe a list of things that they love to do.
- They can be very simple and small things e.g. playing in a pile of leaves, eating ice cream on a sunny day, climbing a tree, dressing up etc.
- Encourage the participants to explain why they enjoy doing those things.

Explanation

The secret of happiness is deceptively simple: *find out what you truly love to do and then direct all of your energies towards doing it.*

If you study the happiest, healthiest, most fulfilled people on the planet, you will find that the vast majority of them have found their passion in life, and then spent their days pursuing it.

When you do what you absolutely love to do, you will find an energy and vigour that seems to be never-ending. You become absorbed in the pleasure of doing what you love and results seem to come without you consciously being aware of it.

Further Activity

Often it is difficult for people to find and express what it is they are passionate about. Here is a useful tool:

- Ask the participants the question: *what would you do if you knew you could not fail?*
- Or, phrased differently: *what would you do if money and time were no object?*
- Or, phrased differently again: *what would you do if you had any wish in the world?*
- Have them write down the answers. Most often this question will reveal what you are truly passionate about.

This question allows the mind to traverse beyond its limiting beliefs to the place where it is free to dream.

Life Lesson/Skill

Find out what you truly love to do, and then direct all of your energies towards doing it. When you do what you love, you will almost certainly find happiness and fulfilment.

When you are inspired
by some great purpose,
some extraordinary project,
all of your thoughts break their bonds:
your mind transcends limitations,
your consciousness expands
in every direction
and you find yourself
in a new, great
and wonderful world.
Dormant forces, faculties
and talents become alive
and you discover yourself
to be a greater person than
you ever dreamed yourself to be.

Anon

18 Contribution

 Life's most persistent and urgent question is: What are you doing for others?
Martin Luther King, Jr.

Toolbox

A large bowl (the larger the better).
A cup of water.

Directions

- Fill the bowl about halfway up with water.
- Now fill the cup about halfway with water.
- Gather the participants around the bowl of water in a circle. Ensure the water is still.

Activity

- Encourage each participant to dip their finger in the cup and then shed a drop of water into the bowl.
- Ask the participants to notice what happens when the drop of water hits the water in the bowl.

Explanation

The actions of each person are like the drop of water. When the drop hits the water, it causes ripples. Notice how the ripples move outwards, affecting the entire surface area of the water. Although sometimes it is hard to imagine, it is important to realize that our actions can make a real difference in the world.

Even the smallest action, the smallest drop, makes a difference. The addition of a single drop increases the size of the body of water, does it not?

When Mother Theresa of Calcutta, India, was asked why she continued with her work, attending to the dying and rescuing children from the streets, when the problem just continued, and when it was suggested that what she did was just a 'drop in the ocean' compared to the many thousands of the poor in need, she answered:

 Yes, it is true, my work is just a small drop in the ocean, but because of my one drop, the entire ocean is bigger.

Be the drop of water causing ripples today. Take action, and make a difference, because you *can*.

The Chinese have a saying: '*A little bit of fragrance always clings to the hand that gives you roses.*'

When you make a difference in the lives of others, you indirectly enrich your own life as a result.

Tip: the above activity can also be conducted by a puddle, pond or lake.

Further Activity

- If you are by the seaside, plan a stop at a nearby beach. Once on the beach, encourage the participants to stand next to each other and walk in a line.
- Encourage them to notice their footprints in the sand. Each person leaves his or her print on the sand, and in doing so, the world is changed forever. It is no longer the same sand, the same beach. So it is with a person's life. Let the footprints remind us of how we can all make a difference in a small way. We can all leave our mark.
- Now lead the participants to the water's edge. Drop a small stone into the water and notice the effect of the ripples as they spread across the water. Encourage the participants to think of a way in which they might increase the ripples.
- Now skim a smooth stone across the water. Each bounce of the stone causes a *new* set of ripples. A stone which is smooth and skims across the water many times causes many sets of ripples in a very short space of time.

We are like skimming stones, causing many sets of ripples at great speed, when we not only make our own ripples, but encourage others to make their own ripples too.

Help and encourage others to contribute too, and the effect is increased tenfold.

Tip: if you are not within a short distance of the ocean or a lake or pond, read out the parable of the starfish below.

Life Lesson/Skill

You can make a difference in the world. Even by doing something small, you can make an impact. By adding your drop, the entire ocean is bigger.

The Starfish Parable

An old man had a habit of early morning walks on the beach. One day, as he looked along the shore, he saw a human figure moving like a dancer. As he came closer he saw that it was a young woman and she was not dancing but was reaching down to the sand, picking up starfish and very gently throwing them into the ocean.

'Young lady,' he asked, 'Why are you throwing starfish into the ocean?'

'The sun is up, and the tide is going out, and if I do not throw them in they will die.'

'But young lady, do you not realise that there are miles and miles of beach and starfish all along it? You cannot possibly make a difference.'

The young woman listened politely, paused and then bent down, picked up another starfish and threw it into the sea, past the breaking waves, saying:

'It made a difference for that one.'

Adapted from *The Star Thrower* by Loren Eiseley

19 Leadership

> ' The individual activity of one man with backbone will do
> more than a thousand men with a mere wishbone.'
> William J.H. Boetcker

Toolbox

CD player and some dance music.

Directions

- Load up the player with some lively dance music.

Activity

- As the music plays, each participant has a turn to lead the group in choosing the dance moves. Perhaps initiate the process by going first.
- Each of the participants has to copy the leader's dance movements. Encourage some outrageous dance moves so that participants can really express themselves!

Tip: avoid a situation where the leader dances in the middle of a circle. This tends to make those who are shy feel more self-conscious.

Explanation

People generally think that you are born a leader. This is not so. Leadership is a skill that can be learned, just like any other skill.

Some of the greatest leaders the world has ever known were withdrawn and felt awkward as a child. Bill Gates, founder of Microsoft, was timid and introverted as a child. Princess Diana was shy and easily intimidated before flourishing into an inspirational figure adored throughout the world.

Leadership does require taking action, however. As shy and introverted as Bill Gates and Princess Diana were, they eventually decided to take action. Leaders step forward and are up for the task. This requires courage. Leadership starts with one small act of courage and ends in the extraordinary empowerment of others.

Everyone has the ability to be a leader. This game is a great example. If participants are doubtful, remind them that for those few moments while dancing, each participant was experiencing being a leader.

Further Activity

- This game is based on the old favourite 'Simon Says'.
- Gather the participants and explain the rules. You, as leader, will instruct them as follows: 'Simon says put your finger on your nose', or 'Simon says put your hands on your knees.' The participants are to copy you. However, if you should say, 'Simon says put your finger on your nose *and* jump up and down', they are to only do the former (put their finger on their nose). They are to ignore any instruction after the word 'and'. Anyone who carries out the instructions after the word 'and' is out of the game.
- After you have been 'Simon' for a few turns, have each of the participants take a turn to lead the group.

Tip: instructions should be given rapidly so that the participants have to pay special attention to the leader. Also, you can make the game harder by including a string of instructions one after another without using the word 'and' e.g. 'Simon says put your hands on your knees, wiggle your bottom, open your mouth and bark like a dog.'

In this game, each participant is again given the opportunity to lead the group. Each opportunity to lead is another step towards building the confidence and skill necessary to be a leader.

Another great skill displayed in this game, and used by many leaders all over the world, is that of modelling. By carefully modelling or simulating the behaviour and conduct of a good leader, we can develop and adopt those same skills.

Life Lesson/Skill

We all have the ability to be a leader. Leadership is a skill that can be learned. Step up and give it a go. The more you practise, the easier it gets!

The difference between a boss and a leader is this:

A boss says, 'Go!' A leader says, 'Let's go!'

E.M. Kelly

20 Persistence and Practice

> The more I practise, the luckier I get.
> Gary Player

Toolbox

One or more spinning tops (or, alternatively, one or more bouncing balls).
Skipping rope (optional).
Paper and pens/pencils as required (optional).

Directions

- Find a large flat surface.

Activity

- Allow each participant to have a turn to spin the spinning top (if a spinning top is unavailable, arrange for each to have a turn bouncing and catching a ball against the wall).
- Ensure that each participant is able to have at least five or six turns, so that they are able to show improvement.

Explanation

Practise, practise, practise.

If you want to improve at anything, you need to practise. Just taking time to do something a few times over and over will show an improvement. For example, notice how performance improved with the spinning top. With just a few practise turns, the participant was able to improve his performance.

Imagine if you practised spinning the top every day!

This is the same in life. Life rewards those people who show the ability to persist with practice.

Don't give up. Some things might take a bit more practise than others. If you are determined to improve, just a little regular practise every day will result in rewards.

Those who excel at a particular skill all know how to practise hard. Olympic gymnasts train for hours every day. They persist. They keep practising.

Tip: The bigger the spinning top, the easier it is to see an improvement.

Further Activity

- There are many other fun games to use as an alternative to the spinning top.
- Try getting the participants to do a handstand and walk on their hands. With a few practice turns, almost everyone will improve dramatically.
- If you have a skipping rope, that is another excellent example. Encourage the participants to count the number of skips they can do – they will usually go up and up!
- Alternatively, have the participants try to stand on one leg. At first, they may battle. First they might be able to stand on one leg for just one second, then two, then three. They will improve quickly with practice.
- Make a 'Persevere Souvenir'. Explain what the word 'persevere' means. Have each participant draw a large circle and within it a picture of himself accomplishing his goal. Cut the circle out and encourage the participant to fasten it onto his jacket or stick it in a place where he can see it every day.

Finally, it is worth considering how people with a great vision never give up. They persist with great determination.

Consider the examples on the next page of how people refused to give up. They just continued until they succeeded.

Don't give up. Practise, practise, practise. If you really want to improve at something, practise hard and regularly, and the results will come.

- During its first year, the Coca-Cola company sold only 400 Cokes.

- Basketballer Michael Jordan was cut/dropped from his high school team.

- Dr Seuss's first children's book, *And to Think that I Saw It on Mulberry Street*, was rejected by 27 publishers. The twenty-eighth publisher, Vanguard Press, has sold over 6 million copies of the book.

- Sir Steve Redgrave was not considered particularly bright at school and was given few chances to 'make a mark' for himself in the world. He chose to try his hand at rowing. Prior to the 1984 Los Angeles Olympics, Steve trained for at least six hours every day for four years, 360 days a year. He won gold at his first Olympics. He put in another four years of similar training for the 1988 Olympics in Seoul, Korea, and again won gold. By 1992 and the Barcelona Games, Steve had put in another four years of dedicated training and won his third gold medal. By 1996, Steve had put in yet another four years of persistence (16 years non-stop!) and was rewarded with his fourth gold medal. No one had won four gold medals consecutively in the Olympic games in an endurance sport. However, that was not enough.

  He went on to train for yet another four years at an even harder intensity (now 20 years on the trot!) for the Sydney Olympics. Then on top of that a year before the Olympics Steve was diagnosed with diabetes, and had to add to his training regime insulin injections six times a day. Determined and resolute, he continued to train and managed to win his fifth Olympic gold medal! Steve is arguably the greatest Olympic athlete of all time. He practised and trained hard for 20 years, six hours a day, 360 days a year.

- In 1905, the University of Bern turned down a doctoral dissertation, as they considered it irrelevant and idealistic. The young student who wrote the dissertation was Albert Einstein, who was disappointed but not outdone. He went on to become one of the greatest scientists that has ever lived.

Many of life's
failures are
people who did
not realise
how close
they were to
success when
they gave up.

Thomas Edison

21 Questions

 The most interesting people in life are those that are the most interested. **9**
Anon

Toolbox

A number of sticky labels or cards.
Sticking tape (if cards are used).
Pens/pencils as required.

Directions

- On the labels write down the names of famous people or characters who are likely to be known to the participants.

Activity

- We have 'Six Honest Serving Men' that serve us very well in life.
- Encourage the participants to guess the identity of those six companions.
- They are indeed: What, Why, When, How, Where and Who (see rhyme on page 49).
- Now play the well-known game of Who Am I?
- Stick a label to the back or forehead of each participant without him seeing it.
- Each participant has to try to find out who he is by asking the other participants questions which can only be answered 'yes' or 'no'.
- After the game, ask the participants:
  o How difficult was it asking only questions which could receive the answer 'yes' or 'no'?
  o How would using the Six Honest Serving Men (so called 'open questions') have helped to make it easier?

Explanation

Children should always be encouraged to ask questions. It is often through the asking and answering of questions that they learn and discover.

Thought, in fact, is nothing but the asking and answering of questions. Think about it…!

Often a child will be confused or intrigued by something. Using the Six Honest Serving Men, they will be able to find out the information they need to reach a better understanding. Young children who have just learned to speak ask many questions (often to the complete exasperation of their parents and teachers!) However, children should always be encouraged to ask questions, or, if the time is not convenient to do so, to keep those questions until a later, more convenient time.

Further Activity

Intelligent people ask questions all the time. In fact, intelligent people just ask *better* questions. When Thomas Edison was inventing the light bulb, he just kept asking: how might there be a better way to make this experiment work? What if I did this? Why did that not work?

Questions are also a great way to change focus.

If you are in a depressed state, you are probably asking depressing questions, like: How come my life is so terrible? Why does that always happen to me? Why can I never get that right?

You can change your focus and your feelings instantly by asking better quality questions. Encourage the participants to write down on a card the following 'Six Power Questions':

1. What am I happy about in my life right now? Or what *could* I be happy about in my life right now?
2. What am I excited about in my life right now? Or what *could* I be excited about in my life right now?
3. What am I proud of in my life right now? Or what *could* I be proud of in my life right now?
4. What am I grateful for in my life right now? Or what *could* I be grateful for in my life right now?

5. What am I really committed to in my life right now? Or what *could* I be really committed to in my life right now?
6. Who do I love? Who loves me?

The 'Six Power Questions' are a terrific way to start the day in a positive state. Encourage the participants to carry the card in their purse or wallet, or stick it up on the wall in the bathroom where they can see it every morning.

Life Lesson/Skill

You have Six Honest Serving Men who are always by your side – What, Why, When, How, Where and Who? Never be afraid to ask questions. There is no such thing as a dumb question.

I keep six honest serving men, they taught me all I knew: their names are What and Why and When and How and Where and Who.

Rudyard Kipling
The Elephant Child

22   The Senses

 Nothing can cure the soul but the senses, just as nothing can cure the senses but the soul.
Oscar Wilde

Toolbox

Blindfold(s).
A range of different items to stimulate the senses (see some suggestions below).
An orange for each participant (optional).

Directions

- Collect a number of small pieces of material of different textures e.g. cardboard, shiny photographic paper, silk, corduroy, sandpaper, terracotta tile, cotton wool etc. These items will be used to explore the sense of touch.
- Collect a range of different scents e.g. spices, scented candles, incense, lavender, flowers, spiced apples, vinegar etc. These will be used to stimulate the sense of smell.
- Collect various materials that can be used to make a sound e.g. empty cans, wind chimes, wooden sticks, Velcro, paper for tearing etc. These will be used to engage the sense of hearing.
- Collect a number of items which the participants can taste e.g. sugar, salt, ice, lemon, savoury biscuits, mild mustard.
- Mix up the items in a pile on a table and cover up the pile with a large cloth.

Activity

- Taking it in turns, have each participant put on the blindfold and approach the table.
- Removing the cloth, get them to touch, smell, hear and taste a few different items and describe them as they go along.
- Now take off the blindfold and see how many items they guessed correctly. Mix up the pile of items again and call up the next participant.

Tip: if there is limited time and you have enough blindfolds, have the participants approach the table in small groups.

Explanation

Each day we experience what is going on around us in our lives through our five senses: sight, touch, hearing, taste and smell.

The purpose of this activity is to encourage the participants to spend time developing the senses – because, as we have said, it is through the senses that we experience life. Therefore, it makes sense that the more developed our senses are, the fuller experience of life we are going to have.

Take time to sit quietly and absorb the world through your five senses. Remember that we are human *beings*, rather than human *doings*. Take time just to 'be', and you will experience that your senses will become heightened – the world will become more alive. In addition, your *doings* or daily activities will become pleasurable and more effortless.

Further Activity

- Hand out an orange to each participant in the group.
- Each participant is to take the orange away to a quiet place and eat it. There is only one rule in this game. They must take at least 20 minutes to eat the orange!
- If the participants are in earshot, read out the questions below, allowing time for reflection between each one. Alternatively, photocopy the questions and have each participant work through each question in turn on their own.

Tip: reading out the questions tends to work better as a means of keeping the focus of the participants on the orange.

- How does the skin of the orange feel in your hands?
- What shape is the orange? Are any areas more pronounced than other areas?
- Are there any discoloured areas on the orange?
- How does it look spinning through the air or rolling down your arm? (Make sure you catch it!)
- How does it smell with the peel on?
- When you shake it can you hear anything?
- How does it feel on the fingers when you break the skin? Wet or dry?
- Taste the first drop of juice on your finger. How does it taste? Bitter or sweet?
- How does it feel on the fingertips when peeling the orange? Does the peel have a smell? Taste the peel. Is it more bitter or sweet than the drop of juice?
- What does it sound like when the peel is pulled off the orange? Is there a ripping sound, or a grating sound? Can you hear a tiny cry?
- Now remove the entire peel. Did some bits come off easier than others? Were you able to get some big bits of peel off? Is there a white skin around the orange now or can you see the individual pieces of orange?
- How does the inside of the peel compare in colour and texture to the outside of the peel?
- Smell the orange now. Does it smell stronger now?
- Peel off a piece of the white skin and taste it. What does it taste like? How does it feel? Rough or smooth on your fingers? How does it feel when you rub it on your cheek?
- Peel off all the white skin now. What do you see? Can you see the veins of each different piece of orange now? Push a piece of the orange. Can you see the juice inside the orange? How does it feel when you prod the piece of orange?
- Break the orange in two now. Does it make a sound when you pull the orange apart?
- Examine the inside of the orange. Is there a hole in the middle or not? What is the colour of the inside? Does it match the colour of the Sun or is it darker or brighter?
- Peel off a piece of the orange. Is it difficult or easy to break a piece off? Does the juice squish onto your hands or does it stay inside the piece of orange?
- Examine the piece of orange. Can you see the veins and fibres of the individual piece? Is the skin transparent? How does the skin feel?
- Pop that piece in your mouth now. Suck on it without breaking the skin. How does that feel? Does it feel moist or dry? Does the piece take up the whole of your mouth?
- Take the piece out and bite off a small bit on the end. What does that taste like? Look inside the orange piece now. What do you see? Does it smell even richer now or just the same?
- Pop the rest of the orange piece in your mouth now and chew on it for a while without swallowing. Close your eyes and focus on the taste in your mouth. Close your ears now. Can you hear your jaw moving down on the orange as you chew it lightly? Does it feel tough or tender when you chew?
- Try not to swallow for as long as possible. Does the taste change over the course of a minute or two?
- Swallow the remains of the orange piece now. Feel how it slides down your throat. Did it feel cool or warm, soft or hard? Place your tongue on the top of your mouth now and then remove it. Do this over and over a few times. What is the taste that is left in your mouth?
- Notice the feeling of impatience as you want to put the rest of the orange in your mouth. Take each piece off carefully and complete the process as above.

You may wish to add some additional questions to the ones above.

At the end of the activity, encourage the participants to share their experiences of eating the orange. Did some participants have different experiences to others?

The participants would have found that, with such a focused attention on their senses during the activity, their experience of eating the orange would have been more pronounced than on prior occasions when they ate an orange. In other words, they would have had a fuller experience.

How might they do this in other activities in their lives?

Finally, older children may find the extract on page 52 interesting (taken from the book *An Evil Cradling* by Brian Keenan). In 1986, Keenan, an English literature professor from Belfast, Northern Ireland, decided to take a break from his native city. He took up a position in the American University in Beirut, Lebanon. Scarcely two weeks after his arrival, he was kidnapped by fundamentalist Muslims and was subsequently imprisoned in a solitary confinement compression chamber, six feet long and four feet wide. Brian was to spend much of his five years' imprisonment in this windowless tomb.

In addition to deep breathing, another way of relaxing is through visualization. When we are resting comfortably, letting our imaginations take us to a place of calm peacefulness and tranquillity is an excellent way of getting rid of stress. Design your own journey to a place that is serene, quiet and beautiful. You will find that your worries drift away.

Life Lesson/Skill

We all get stressed or anxious from time to time. Remember that focusing on deep breaths and calming scenes in times of stress can help you relax and overcome your anxiety.

Breathing and Visualization Experience

You may wish to play relaxing music in the background while you read out the following directions:

Sit or lie in a comfortable position. Gently close your eyes and take a deep breath in and out… Breathe in deeply again now, and as you breathe out, you breathe out a warm, peaceful feeling into every part of your body…Imagine in your mind a warm summer's day…You are lying in a beautiful field of lush green grass…As you look up into the glorious sky, you see a large, fluffy cloud passing by…As you watch the cloud, it begins to float down and drift towards you…The cloud nestles next to you on the ground…You notice how soft and fluffy it is…You climb on top of the cloud…Feel how comfortable it is, like lying in a field of cotton…You take a deep breath in and out and feel so relaxed now, lying on your cloud…The cloud gently lifts off the ground and soon you are drifting along effortlessly in the sky…Before long you come across a beautiful rainbow…The cloud is surrounded by the rainbow now…All around you are the most enchanting colours…You drift into the colour pink and the whole cloud becomes a pink colour…Fill your lungs with the pink colour now…Notice how you are feeling…You drift into the colour blue and notice that the cloud has now also become that colour…Take a deep breath in and breathe in the blue…Notice how that makes you feel…You drift into a golden colour and you are bathed in a warm, rich feeling which makes you feel so content…You are out of the cloud now, but that wonderful feeling is still with you…You drift slowly back down to earth now, knowing that feeling is available to you at any time…Your cloud delivers you gently onto the soft field and you watch it move slowly up into the sky and away in the distance…When you are ready, open your eyes and stretch… Notice how relaxed you feel.

When I look back on all these worries, I remember the story of the old man who said on his deathbed that he had had a lot of trouble in his life, most of which never happened.

Winston Churchill

24 Change

Change is inevitable; growth is intentional.
Glenda Cloud

Toolbox

Photographs or yearbook, as directed below (optional).
Pen and paper (optional).

Directions

- If you have time for preparation, arrange for the participants to each bring to the group a photograph of them that is a few years old. It could even be a photograph of when they were a baby. Alternatively get a yearbook or a class photo from a previous year.
- If there is no time for such preparation, play the alternative game suggested below.

Activity

- Have the participants review the photos and point out the changes with respect to each person. In what ways have they changed?
- Alternatively, pick some of the participants from the group to stand in front of the group. Have the other participants carefully view the selected participants. Tell them that in a moment they will have to close their eyes and each selected participant will change something about themselves e.g. undo a button, undo shoelaces, remove a layer of clothing.
- Now get the viewing participants to close their eyes for one minute. Have each selected participant make a change.
- Encourage the viewing participants to guess what changes have been made by each selected participant.

Tip: This game can be adapted, depending on the age and numbers of the participants e.g. for older participants, ensure the changes are more subtle; for younger participants, make the changes more obvious.

Explanation

Each year children will face change in their lives. They may simply graduate to a new class in school where they will be faced with a new teacher, a different classroom or a new set of subjects to learn. They may change friends. Very often they will change towns and go to a new school in a completely different environment. Change can be quite daunting at times.

But change is all around us. The seasons change constantly. Each day the sun is out for longer/shorter than the previous day. Each day we get older. Each day the plants grow a little more. Each day the winds change direction and speed, the ocean's currents shift the seabed and the sand-dunes change shape.

Change is a part of life and should be embraced.

Children are usually more adaptable than adults. They certainly embrace new trends, technologies and ideas more readily than adults! What children fear most about change, however, is the uncertainty that it brings.

Encourage the participants to see that change can be a good thing. Very often as things change they get better and improve. For example, perhaps discuss how new technologies have improved our lives and made them easier.

A new environment usually brings opportunity – opportunity to meet new people, bring in new ideas, see new things and grow as individuals.

Further Activity

- Ask for suggestions from the participants of some things they would like to change about the world e.g. less pollution, more peace etc.

- Now encourage the participants to think of something in their lives they wish to change for the better. It does not have to be a large change necessarily. Get them to write it down on a piece of paper.
- Discuss with the participants how they intend to bring about this change e.g. do they have to make a change in attitude or behaviour?
- Encourage them to write down all the positive consequences of making the change and all the negative consequences of *not* making the change.
- Discuss how you might support each participant with the proposed change.

As mentioned above, with change comes opportunity. We each have the opportunity to make positive changes in our own life. If we are unable to change something we don't like, we can change our attitude towards it.

But change requires a decision. It requires a strong commitment to alter our behaviour or our attitude. If we are not truly committed it is unlikely the change will be a lasting one.

Furthermore, the more positive consequences there are for making a change, and the more negative consequences there are for *not* making the change, the greater the chances of making the change successfully. Therefore, the more support and encouragement we can give children when making a change the easier it will be to make the change.

Life Lesson/Skill

Change is a constant part of life. We need to keep changing as individuals in order to grow and develop. Do not fear change. Very often change can bring positive results.

Change has a considerable psychological impact on the human mind.

To the fearful it is threatening because
it means that things may get worse.

To the hopeful it is encouraging because things may get better.

To the confident it is inspiring because the
challenge exists to make things better.

King Whitney, Jr.

25 Disabilities and Weaknesses

 No one is perfect – that's why pencils have erasers.
Anon

Toolbox

Access to the internet or a library (optional).

Directions

- Arrange for the participants to be seated in a circle.

Activity

- Ask each participant to think of one thing they are good at and one thing they are not good at.
- Now ask each participant in turn to stand up and introduce themselves and then state out loud the thing they are good at and the thing they are not so good at e.g. 'My name is James. I am good at playing soccer but not so good at sums.'

Tip: It is important that each participant stick to this formula. There may be some participants who will only wish to mention a strength and not a weakness. Others may only wish to focus on their weaknesses. The above recital will help the participants to have a more balanced view of themselves.

Explanation

Nobody is perfect. We all have some things we are good at and some things we are not good at. We all have our strengths and weaknesses, abilities and disabilities.

Since we all have weaknesses or disabilities, no one should be ridiculed or excluded by virtue of a particular weakness or disability. That would be unfair, wouldn't it?

Further Activity

- Set a fun task for the participants. Have them research online or in the library any person who has achieved great things despite the fact that they had a disability.
- Examples could include disabled athletes Dame Tanni Grey-Thompson, Natalie du Toit or Oscar Pretorious, authors Shirley Cheng and James Joyce, inventors Alexandra Graham Bell, Thomas Edison and Henry Ford, scientists Stephen Hawking and Albert Einstein, mathematician Pythagoras, artist Leonardo da Vinci, singers Stevie Wonder, Ray Charles, Billy Joel, Elton John, John Cougar Mellencamp and John Lennon, actors Michael J. Fox, Peter Falk and Marlee Matlin, heroine Joan of Ark, US Presidents Thomas Jefferson, Abraham Lincoln, Franklin Roosevelt, George Washington and John F. Kennedy, academic Irving King Jordan, humanitarian Helen Keller, senator Joseph Robert Kerrey, diver Greg Louganis, baseballer Jim Abbott, King Alexander the Great, boxer Mohammad Ali, pilot Sir Douglas Bader, composer Ludwig van Beethoven or generals Napoleon Bonaparte and Julius Caesar.

- Ask them to report back after a short break or the next day and inform the other participants of the results of their research.
- Discuss how even those with a severe weakness or disability can accomplish extraordinary things.

Just because someone has a weakness or disability does not mean that they are any less important as a person. As the above activity illustrates, those with severe weaknesses or disabilities can and do achieve tremendous feats every day.

Life Lesson/Skill

Nobody is perfect. We all have strengths and weaknesses, abilities and disabilities of some kind. Just because someone has a weakness or a disability does not mean they are any less important as a person.

A true friend knows
your weaknesses
but shows you your strengths;
feels your fears but
fortifies your faith;
sees your anxieties
but frees your spirit;
recognises your disabilities
but emphasizes
your possibilities.

William Arthur Ward

50 Life skills

GAMES FOR AGES 7 AND UPWARDS

26 Getting Rid of 'I Can't'

 They can conquer who believe they can.
Virgil

Toolbox

Pad of paper and pens/pencils as required.
One shoebox.
One spade (helpful).
Thick marker (optional).

Directions

- Hand out a piece of paper and pen/pencil to each participant.

Activity

- Get each participant to make a heading on the top of the page that reads 'I Can'ts'.
- Now get each participant to make a list of all the things that they 'can't' do. For example, a participant may write 'I can't kick a soccer ball in the air more than three times in a row; I can't do sums; I can't get Debbie to like me; I can't ride a bike; I can't do a handstand etc.
- Allow this to proceed for at least 10 or 15 minutes.
- Now get each participant to fold their papers in half and put them into an empty shoebox.
- Put the lid on the box and announce that you are all going outside.
- In a suitable place outside, and with the help of a spade or similar instrument, dig a hole big enough to fit the shoebox. Usually, each participant will want to help with the digging!
- Place the box of 'I Can'ts' in the hole and get each participant to throw sand on the box until it is covered.
- If the participants are old enough, you may choose to deliver a eulogy (funeral speech):
  'Friends, we are gathered here today to honour the memory of "I Can't". While with us here on Earth, he touched everyone's lives, some more than others. We have provided "I Can't" with a final resting place. He is survived by "I Can", "I Will", and "I'm Going To". They are not as well known as their relative – but with a little help, perhaps they will make a greater mark on the world. May everyone here pick up their lives and move forward in his absence. May "I Can't" rest in peace forever.'
- Return inside, and hold a wake. Celebrate the passing of 'I Can't' with some popcorn or fruit juice. Bid 'I Can't' farewell with the words: 'To "I Can't" – may he rest in peace' and make a celebratory toast to "I Can", "I Will" and "I'm Going To".

Tip: you can use a lighter to burn the pieces of paper if you are unable to dig a hole in the garden, but this should be carefully controlled. Alternatively, encourage the participants to simply throw the pieces of paper into the bin.

Explanation

We can all do with putting 'I Can't' to rest. Sometimes, particularly when we are a child, it seems as if there is a lot we can't do. We keep hanging out with our friend 'I Can't'. For one thing, we are always being told what we can't do, right?

If we keep getting told we can't do things, we build up an 'I Can't' attitude, and we may spend the rest of our lives with our 'I Can't' so that he becomes our best friend and next-door neighbour! Or worse – he moves right in!

If you 'Can't', you 'Won't'.

Get rid of 'I Can't'. Replace it with 'I Can', 'I Will', and 'I'm Going To'. They will serve you much better as companions on the journey of life.

- As a reminder that we have put 'I Can't' to rest, cut out a large tombstone and with the thick marker write 'I Can't' at the top, RIP in the middle and the date at the bottom. Stick it up on the wall. When a participant forgets and says 'I Can't', point to the tombstone. Remind the participant that 'I Can't' is dead, and get him to rephrase the statement.
- To reinforce the message, encourage the participants to write out a list of all the things they *can* do (no matter how insignificant), and celebrate this with applause as each participant reads the list out to the group.

Life Lesson/Skill

Put 'I Can't' to rest once and for all. 'I Can', 'I Will' and 'I'm Going To' will serve you much better on the journey of life.

Whether you
think you can
or
whether you
think you can't
you're right.

Henry Ford

27   Individuality

 What is genius – but the power of expressing a new individuality?
Elizabeth Barrett Browning

Toolbox

None.

Directions

- See below.

Activity

- Have the participants stand up and form a circle. Explain that you are going to call out a variety of numbers and the participants must arrange themselves in groups of those numbers. So if you call the number three, then everyone must organize themselves in groups of threes. Between the commands, the participants need to move around so that they don't form groups with the same people.
- Have a few practise turns, so that the participants get the idea. Those who are left out are just to stand still and wait for the next command before rejoining the game.
- Now explain that you are going to play for real. If anyone is left out of a group this time, they are out of the game and must go to the side of the room.
- The game continues until you have only a few participants left and you call out the number two. Someone loses and the couples that are left are the winners.

Explanation

We have all had the experience of feeling 'left out' in our lives. Sometimes we desperately want to be part of the 'in group', even when the 'in group' are not necessarily people we would ordinarily spend time with.

But it is important to remember that we cannot be part of every group all of the time. Just because we are not in a group does not mean that we need to feel 'left out'. It is perfectly okay to be on your own. In fact, sometimes it is good to stand out from the crowd, to be different, and to be an independent thinker, rather than a person who simply follows others like a flock of sheep.

Further Activity

- Have all the participants sit down on the floor. Read out the statements on page 65. If the participants agree with the statement, or it applies to them, they are to stand up.
- Those participants who are standing should remain standing until they disagree with a statement, in which case they should sit down. Encourage the participants to notice who is in agreement with them and who is not.
- How did they feel when they were not part of the group standing up? Did they ever feel uncomfortable being part of a group? Were they ever pleased not to be part of a group?
- Afterwards, take some time to discuss with the participants when it is good to be part of a group, and when it is not. Think of some examples of people who did not mind being 'left out', who chose to stand out from the crowd and think differently. An example might be Galileo Galilei, who first proposed that the Earth was flat, the Wright brothers who were branded as 'freaks' before taking the first flight, or the ugly duckling in Hans Christian Anderson's book.

Life Lesson/Skill

We all feel left out at times. We cannot be part of every group all of the time. Being in the 'in crowd' is not as important as you might think. It is more important to be true to yourself, to follow your heart and develop your own identity.

Statement List

1. I have blue eyes.
2. My favourite colour is red.
3. I have a pet dog/cat.
4. I love mathematics.
5. Football is my favourite sport.
6. I once threw litter onto the ground.
7. My favourite food is pizza.
8. I once cheated on a test.
9. I would like to be president/prime minister.
10. I can cook eggs and bacon.
11. I own a pair of jeans.
12. My favourite singer is Eminem.
13. I have long hair.
14. I wear my watch on my left hand.
15. I can speak more than one language.
16. I own a pair of rollerblades.
17. I have a pair of Nike trainers
18. Both my grandparents are still alive.
19. I was once in a fight.
20. My favourite drink is Coke.
21. I am wearing the colour blue.
22. I am not wearing glasses/spectacles.
23. I once failed a test.
24. I have tried fishing.
25. I once told a lie.
26. I love ice cream.
27. My first name is shorter than five letters.
28. I like swimming.
29. I have a coin in my pocket.
30. I know all the words of the national anthem.

No man
ever yet
became great
by imitation.

Samuel Johnson

28 Labels

> Labels are for filing. Labels are for clothing. Labels are not for people.
> Martina Navratilova

Toolbox

Six to eight tin cans with labels removed.
Two different sets of home-made labels for the cans.
Two small price tags for each can.
A glue stick or sticking tape.
Different coloured pens.
White sticky labels or name tags (one for each participant) (optional).

Directions

- Decorate the home-made labels with outrageous names and pictures that will appeal to children and attract their attention e.g. Paul's Pickled Prunes, Mary's Magic Marshmellows, Jane's Jumping Jellies, Norman's Speckled and Honey Fried Wigworms, Simon's Special Scandinavian Snails (the labels should vary in terms of desirability and appeal of the contents).
- Place one set of the new home-made labels on the cans.

Activity

- Display the cans on a table before the participants.
- Pick up each can and read out the label aloud.
- Explain to the participants that you are now going to have an auction. One by one, the participants will bid on the cans according to how much they would be willing to pay for each can. Write the highest bid for each can on a price tag and affix to the top of the can.
- Now remove all the labels and paste on the second set of labels, altering which cans receive appealing and unappealing labels. Place the first set of home-made labels under the cans.
- Take a second round of bids and note the highest bid on a second price tag in a different coloured ink.
- Pose the following questions to the participants:
  o Did they bid higher on the cans with labels for good-tasting foods?
  o Did changing the label on the can change what was really inside?
  o Do we really know what is inside these cans?
  o What did changing the labels make us do in our minds?

Explanation

We tend to label people just as we do cans. We might call them 'dumb' or 'thick' or 'cute'. Often we do this without really knowing what's on the inside.

Further Activity

- Select from page 68 a label for each sticker, and ensure that there is at least one label for each participant.
- Divide the participants up into two teams.
- Stick a label onto the forehead of each participant without letting them see what the label says.
- Now gather the participants. Explain that they are to pretend that they are about to go on a weekend camping trip together and they are to discuss the arrangements e.g. where they will go and what they will do.
- They are to react to one another according to the labels stuck on their forehead. However, they are not to say what the label is. (For example, the participant reacting to the label 'bully' could say, 'Must you pick on

everyone?' or 'Stop throwing your weight around.')

- After playing the game for five to ten minutes encourage each participant to guess what is written on their label.

Discuss with the participants how it felt to have a label, and how it felt to have people react according to that label. How do people get labelled in real life? Is this a good thing?

Life Lesson/Skill

Life Lesson/Skill: Sometimes we can be quick to label others. Do we really know what they are like on the inside? Be aware that labels may not be true reflections of character and can in turn influence how people feel about themselves.

Labels

- o Bad tempered
- o Very funny person
- o Bully
- o Always in trouble
- o Smart
- o Super friendly
- o Mr/Miss Popularity
- o Never does a thing right
- o Depressed
- o Leader
- o Shy
- o Caring person
- o Joker
- o Reliable
- o Boring
- o Liar

29 Communication

> Communication is a skill that you learn. It's like riding a bike or typing. If you are willing to work at it, you can rapidly improve the quality of every part of your life.
>
> Brian Tracy

Toolbox

A coin.
A ball.
A suitable number of chairs (optional).

Directions

- Divide the participants into two teams.

Activity

- Have the teams sit in two rows facing each other.
- Position yourself between the two teams and at one end so that both participants at the end of the row can see your hands.
- At the other end of the rows, place the ball halfway between the last two participants.
- Each participant is to close his eyes, except for the two participants at the end of the rows nearest you. Flip the coin into the air and show it to the two participants who are at the head of the rows nearest you. If the coin shows heads, they are then to squeeze the hand of the person next to them. When each participant feels the squeeze, they are to pass on the squeeze down the row. When the last participant in the row feels the squeeze, he opens his eyes and grabs the ball.
- The team that grabs the ball first wins a point. When a point is won, the teams rotate towards the front, with the first person in the row going to the back and the other members of the team moving forward. This allows everyone in the team to have a chance to play in all positions.
- If the coin comes up tails, then no squeeze is to be sent. However, sometimes the first participant in the row will misread the coin and send the wrong message down the row. If the message goes all the way down the row and the ball is grabbed, then that team loses a point. No rotation is made in this case.
- If the participant who is at the head of the row sends a false message and makes a sound that indicates he has made a mistake, that team automatically loses a point even if the message does not make it all the way to the end of the row.

Explanation

Communication is a vital tool in all walks of life. Our ability to communicate clearly and openly deeply affects the way we interact with one another.

However, often when we communicate with one another, the messages we send are misunderstood. This can be because sometimes we send the wrong message (this is how rumours start). Or it could be because the message is not clear and is misunderstood. Finally, it could be because the person receiving the message is not listening carefully to the message we are trying to send.

Communication is about the sending and receiving of messages. It takes both to be a good communicator.

Try to ensure that you understand what you mean before explaining it to another. Then, try to ensure that the message that you send is clear. As the receiver of a message, be sure to pay careful attention to the communicator and be open to their message.

Further Activity

- Arrange for the participants to sit on chairs in a circle, if possible.
- Explain to the participants that they are all going on a journey to the South Pole.
- Each participant is permitted to take along a certain object or item on the trip.

- Each participant has a turn to state the following: 'I am going to the South Pole and I am taking a ... with me.'
- Explain that you, as the expedition leader, will then decide whether they are able to take along the chosen object to the South Pole. You will answer by saying either 'yes' or 'no'.
- The aim of the game is for the participants to spot the rule behind the decision. In this case, the decision is based on whether or not the participant has his legs crossed during his turn. If the participant has his legs crossed during his turn, he is able to take that chosen object or item to the South Pole along with him on his trip.
- Begin the game by illustrating a successful example.

Tip: if the game goes on too long give clues by exaggerating the crossing and uncrossing of legs. Be aware that if the participants are seated on the ground, the secret rule will be discovered more easily.

We communicate in a host of ways. Experts in the study of communication have said that only 7 per cent of our communication is verbal. This means that 93 per cent of our communication is non-verbal! In order to communicate effectively, we therefore need to be aware of the non-verbal communication that is going on all around us.

Become aware of the totality of the features of a person when he or she is communicating with you. Observe their eyes, their facial expression, the tilt of their head, and the way they hold their shoulders. Are their arms folded or at the sides? Do they make gestures while speaking? All of these factors give us an indication of how someone is feeling and an insight into the significance and meaning of their communication.

Life Lesson/Skill

Communication is a vital skill in our being effective in our daily lives. As the communicator, try to ensure that the messages you send are clear, to avoid misunderstanding. As the receiver, listen carefully to the message being communicated and pay special attention to the body language of the communicator.

The most important
thing in communication
is to hear
what isn't being said.

Peter Drucker

30 Compassion

 Never criticise another man until you have walked a mile in his moccasins.
American Indian Proverb

Toolbox

Pad of paper and pens/pencils as required.
Newspaper clippings covering a range of events (optional).

Directions

- Have the participants take off their shoes.

Activity

- Each participant is to take one of his shoes and place it on a piece of paper.
- Participants should attempt to trace around the border of the shoe, ensuring that their pens or pencils do not leave the page and their eyes never leave the shoe. They should sign their names on the bottom right corner of the page.
- Encourage the participants to swap drawings with another.
- Encourage the participants to notice the differences in the shape of the shoes. Are there many differences? What do the differences tell us about one another?
- Now encourage the participants to swap pairs of shoes with another. The participants should try them on and walk around in them for a while. How does it feel to walk in another's shoes?

Explanation

What is compassion? It is not really feeling sorry for another. Nor is it feeling pity for another. It is more like empathy – feeling *with* another. It is an *awareness* and *understanding* of the needs of another in a particular situation.

The desire to help others who are less fortunate than ourselves or just going through a hard time arises from our sense of compassion. We are all in need of compassion at some time in our lives.

Sometimes it is hard to imagine what another person may be feeling at a particular time. If we imagine ourselves 'walking in their shoes' it helps us to form the understanding and awareness that gives rise to compassion. It helps us to see things from their point of view and imagine how they feel.

Further Activity

- Distribute a newspaper clipping to each participant.
- Tip: the clippings should describe a broad range of events, such as accidents, fires, illnesses, honours, awards, concerts, sporting achievements, births and deaths.
- Ask the participants to read the clippings and write down as many feeling words as necessary to describe the emotions of the people involved. If there are several different perspectives referred to, ask participants to identify the various people's feelings (for example, if the captain of a winning team is interviewed, try to identify how the losing captain must feel).
- Encourage participants to share their clippings and explain what they think the particular person(s) must be feeling.
- Alternatively, read the Parable of the Stone on page 73.

Discuss with the participants why it is important to be compassionate towards others. What are the things we can do to find out more about how another person feels?

Compassion is the gateway to love. Be sensitive to the needs and feelings of others. Try to imagine walking in their shoes and seeing things from their perspective.

Parable of the Stone

A wise woman who was travelling in the mountains found a precious stone on the bed of a small river stream.

The next day while on her way she met another traveller who was tired and hungry, and the wise woman opened her bag to share her food with the traveller. The hungry traveller saw the precious stone in her bag and asked the woman to give it to him.

She did so without hesitation.

The traveller left rejoicing in his good fortune. He knew the stone was worth enough to give him security for a lifetime. But, a few days later, he came back and returned the stone to the wise woman.

'I have been thinking,' said the traveller.

'I know how valuable this stone is, but I give it back to you in the hope that you can give me something even more precious. Give me what you have within you that enabled you to give me this stone.'

How far you go in life depends on your being tender with the young, compassionate with the aged, sympathetic with the striving, and tolerant of the weak and strong, because someday you will have been all of these.

George Washington Carver

31 Creativity

' We are all cups, constantly and quietly being filled. The trick is knowing
how to tip ourselves over and let the beautiful stuff out. '
Ray Bradbury

Toolbox

CD player with dance music (optional).
Poster pages and marker (optional).

Directions

- Arrange for the participants to stand in a circle.

Activity

- Arrange for the participants to play the dancing game in Chapter 19. Each participant should be given the opportunity to create his own dance routine or movements before the other participants while the other participants copy him.
- Alternatively, have each participant in turn make a funny face. Explain that this face is a 'mask'. On your instruction, have the participant take off the mask by running his hand over his face in a swift movement and fling it across the room to another participant, who immediately puts on the 'mask'. By running his hand over his face, that participant changes the facial expression of the 'mask', before flinging it across the room to another participant on your instruction.

Explanation

Creativity is the ability to be creative. We all have the ability to create. It is part of our nature. Everybody can be an artist, a cook or a dancer.

Does it really matter if our creation is 'good' or 'bad'? Who decides what is 'good' or 'bad'?

Discuss the fact that even the most expensive artworks in the world are considered by some to be 'genius' and others to be 'ordinary'. Some foods are described as 'delicacies' in some countries and 'inedible' in others.

What matters is that we harness our creativity. The more we use it, the more it develops and grows.

Further Activity

- Divide the participants into groups of four to eight.
- Appoint a leader for each group. The leader is the 'window dresser'.
- Explain to the window dresser that he is arranging a window design to promote a new range e.g. summer sports goods or beach goods or ski gear or camping gear or hardware. The other participants in his group are the 'mannequins' or dummies.
- Have the window dresser bring the mannequins into the shop window and use them in the display. Encourage the window dresser to bend the arms and knees of the mannequins and adjust their heads, facial expressions and hands so as to have them engaged in activity that will display the new range.
- Once the window dresser is finished, encourage the other participants to guess the new range.
- Discuss with the participants the concept of 'brainstorming'. Write a number of topics on separate poster sheets or on a board. The topics should be a question or a problem e.g. climate change, drought, hunger, world peace. Encourage the participants to 'brainstorm' ways of solving or addressing these issues. Explain that *all* ideas are welcome, regardless of how far-fetched they might seem. There are no 'right' or 'wrong' ideas.

Tip: if there are only a few participants in the group, give each participant the opportunity to be the window dresser.

Our ability to come up with creative solutions to problems or challenges is often enhanced in a group. By 'bouncing' ideas off one another we can create solutions or ideas we might not have come up with alone.

Life Lesson/Skill

We all have the ability to be creative. It is in being creative that we discover ourselves. The more we use our creative power, the more it develops and grows.

Top 10 Creative Rules of Thumb

1. The best way to get great ideas is to get lots of ideas and throw the bad ones away.
2. Create ideas that are 15 minutes ahead of their time…not light years ahead.
3. Always look for a second 'right' answer.
4. If at first you don't succeed, take a break.
5. Write down your ideas before you forget them.
6. If everyone says you are wrong, you're one step ahead. If everyone laughs at you, you're two steps ahead.
7. The answer to your problem already exists. You need to ask the right question to reveal the answer.
8. Ask better quality questions and you will get better quality answers.
9. Never solve a problem from its original perspective.
10. Visualize your problem as solved before solving it.

The very essence of
creativity is novelty;

and hence we have
no standard
by which
to judge it.

Carl Rogers

50 Life skills

**GAMES FOR AGES
8 AND UPWARDS**

32 Perspectives/Beliefs

 We don't see things as they are; we see them as we are.
Anais Nin

Toolbox

Different coloured transparent sheets (Perspex or other coloured transparent plastic material, such as cellophane), or various plastic glasses/spectacles with different coloured lenses (usually obtainable from a local toy shop at little cost).
One drinking glass (optional).

Directions

- If the glasses are obtainable, get the participants to put on the glasses. If not, cut the coloured transparent sheets into face-size sections.

Activity

- Encourage each person to wear the glasses or look through the different coloured sheets and describe what they see.
- How is the world different? In what ways was the world different when they took the glasses off again?

Explanation

We all look through the world through different glasses. If we wear red glasses, or look through transparent red lenses, the whole world will appear red.

The glasses or lenses through which we look represent our beliefs. What are beliefs? Beliefs are really feelings of certainty which you have about various things e.g. I believe that going to school is important.

Whatever the nature of our beliefs is, so that will effect what we see in the world. For example, if we believe that the world is a terrible place filled with 'bad people', we will wear 'terrible-place-with-bad-people' glasses, and so this will tend to become our reality. We will begin to see bad people all over the place, which will further strengthen our belief. We will also begin to act accordingly e.g. we will trust no one, and treat other people badly because we believe that the world is filled with bad people.

On the other hand, if we believe that the world is an exciting place full of opportunity, we will wear 'exciting-place-full-of-opportunity' glasses, and this will tend to become our reality. We will also begin to act accordingly e.g. we will be on the look out for opportunities all the time because we believe that they exist and because of this we will be more likely to find them.

Because people have various different coloured glasses on, they have different beliefs about the world.

Encourage kids to develop empowering beliefs about themselves and the world, and they will begin to experience the benefits of these beliefs as their reality.

Tip: If you can persuade the participants, get them to wear the coloured glasses for an entire morning or afternoon – this will really help them to understand the lesson! (In order to do this, tell them that they look really cool in those glasses!)

Further Activity

A more advanced lesson to be learned here is that what we see is not always the reality – it is only a representation of the reality. In other words, if the participant wore red-coloured glasses, they will realize afterwards that in fact the world is not all red-coloured at all – it was just their representation of reality at that time.

- Fill up a glass with water and place it on the table. Does the participant see it as half empty or half full? Whatever their belief is, that will be their representation of reality at that time.
- You may wish to get each participant to write down some of their beliefs about the world – this tends to reveal some interesting and, at times, astonishing beliefs, which are continuously impacting on the actions of the participant in his life. You may then wish to work with the participant to reinforce the empowering beliefs, and replace the disempowering beliefs.[1]
- You may wish to begin a discussion around whether or not holding certain disempowering beliefs actually serves a child or helps them in any way. For instance, if a child believes for some reason that all fat people are stupid, does this belief really serve them? How will this affect the way that they treat fat people in the future? What if one day they met a fat person who was really clever? What if everyone in the world started believing that all fat people were stupid?

Life Lesson/Skill

We all look at the world through different coloured glasses. Whatever coloured glasses you look through, this will affect what you see and experience. The glasses represent our beliefs. If you have positive beliefs about the world, this will tend to become your reality.

Better keep yourself
clean and bright;

You are the window
through which you must
see the world

George Bernard Shaw

33   **Peer Pressure**

 When push comes to shove, think independently.
Chuck Swindall

Toolbox

One quart-size or large glass jar with a mouth on it that is slightly smaller than a hard-boiled egg (fruit juice bottles or milk bottles will also suffice)(optional).
A minimum of two peeled hard-boiled eggs (optional).
A match (optional).
A small piece of notepaper (optional).

Directions

- Divide the participants into two groups, Group 1 and Group 2.

Activity

- Have the Group 1 participants stand and form a circle in the middle of the room.
- Ask the Group 2 participants to stand and form another circle around the Group 1 circle.
- Encourage the Group 2 participants to move in a circular direction around the Group 1 participants. When you say 'Stop', each Group 2 participant is to come to a stop opposite a Group 1 participant.
- The Group 2 participant is to make a request or series of requests, such as 'Can I borrow your new bike?', 'Can I borrow your science homework?', 'Why don't we steal Mary's lunch?', 'Would you like a ride home with me today?', or 'Why don't you try just a sip?' before moving round in a clockwise direction.
- The Group 1 participant is to think of a number of ways of firmly saying 'No', such as 'No, thank you', 'No, sorry', 'No, I can't do that', 'I would rather not do that, thank you', 'No can do' or 'That's not my deal'.
- Have the groups switch and conduct the same activity again.

  Tip: if the group is small, have the Group 2 participants ask several questions of the Group 1 participants, or if the group is large, limit them to a single question before moving.

Explanation

Sometimes it is hard for us to say 'no'. This is especially so when we are in a group of friends and we feel pressured into doing something. It takes courage and confidence not to give in.

But remember to be true to who you are. If you would rather not participate in an activity because it makes you feel uncomfortable, say 'no'. No one has the right to make you do something which is illegal, dangerous or harmful to you.

Discuss with the participants how there are many ways of saying 'no'. Different situations call for different ways of saying 'no'. Experiment with a few variations and use the one that feels right for you in the circumstances.

Further Activity

- Place the glass bottle and the peeled hard-boiled egg on a table in front of the room.
- Select a volunteer to come forward. Encourage him to place the small end of the egg on the top of the bottle and try to push the egg into the bottle. The top of the bottle should be just smaller than the egg so that this should not be possible without breaking the egg.
- Now take the paper and roll it up. Hold it in a horizontal position and light one end of the paper. Once the paper is lit, drop it into the bottle.
- Immediately place the second hard-boiled egg (or the original one if it is still whole) onto the top of the bottle. Ensure that the narrower end of the egg is placed on the top of the bottle.
- Very quickly the egg will be sucked down into the bottle. Do not be concerned if there is very little

flame. Not much is needed to complete the activity (the scientific explanation is that the burning paper consumes all the oxygen, creating a vacuum and sucking the egg down into the bottle).

It is harder to say 'no' when you are stuck in a certain situation or environment, and are continuously being pressured. When the heat is on, you can easily get 'sucked in', like the egg. If you are stuck in a situation or environment where you feel you are being 'sucked in', remove yourself from the situation or environment as soon as possible. Discuss with the participants how they may do this in a variety of situations.

> **Life Lesson/Skill**
>
> No one has the right to make you do anything which is illegal, dangerous or harmful to you. Learn to say 'no' with confidence. If those around you do not respect your decision, remove yourself from that situation or environment as soon as possible.

34 Thinking Outside the Box

> " A mind stretched by a new idea never returns to its original dimensions. "
> Oliver Wendell Holmes

Toolbox

Pad of paper and pens/pencils as required.
Paper clip and coat hanger (optional).

Directions

- Get each participant to draw nine dots on a piece of paper as seen below:

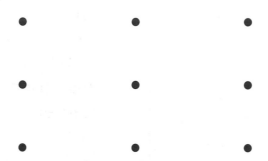

Activity

- Get each participant to try to connect all nine dots by using only four straight lines and without lifting their pen or pencil from the page. Try to ensure there is no peeking!
- The answer is on page 131.

Explanation

Those who were unable to complete the activity successfully were probably thinking that they needed to stay 'inside the box', right? In this case, however, you had to think 'outside the box' to solve the puzzle.

Sometimes in life you will need to think outside the box. We are so used to thinking that there are rules for thinking. The only rule for thinking is that *there are no rules*!

People who came up with great ideas thought 'outside of the box'. People such as Einstein, Leonardo da Vinci, and Galileo thought from another angle, from another point of view. There is always another way of looking at things.

Tip: ask yourself a great question - how can I look at this differently?

Further Activity

- Get the participants to think of how many uses there are for a paper clip. Encourage the participants to use their imagination, with a prize for the most bizarre suggestion! Suggestions are found on page 131–32 of this book.
- Alternatively, listed on page 86 are 40 randomly generated words. Participants should try to find as many uses/associations, as they can between a coat hanger and each of the listed words. You will find some suggestions at page 132 of this book.

Life Lesson/Skill

Sometimes life requires us to look at things differently to find the answer. Try to look at things 'outside the box'. Remember that the only rule to thinking is that there are no rules!

Tennis ball	Cereal bowl
Rain	Flashlight
Medal	Pepper
Telephone	Wig
Shell	Bell
Guitar	CD
Clown	Oak tree
Foot	Tortoise
Potato	Goat
Handkerchief	Singing
Hat	Surfboard
Onion	Eagle
Plant	Hot-air balloon
Pencil	Cowboy
Planets	Telescope
Fork	Carpet
Coffee	Sun
Watch	Saw
Ice	Cardigan
Kangaroo	Yacht

35   **Focus**

 At any given moment in time what we experience depends on what we focus on.
Anthony Robbins

Toolbox

A straight-backed chair (optional).

Directions

- Prepare the participants by getting them to close their eyes.

Activity

- Get the participants to open their eyes, look around the room and make a note of all the objects in the room which are red.
- Now get the participants to close their eyes and with their eyes still closed, get them to try to remember all the objects in the room which were blue.

Explanation

The purpose of this game is to illustrate that what we focus on, we tend to get. At first, we chose to focus on all the objects in the room which were red. So our brains focused on all the red objects and we did not take notice of any blue objects, even though we obviously 'saw' blue objects when we looked around the room.

Because we were focused on the red objects, we simply did not take in any of the blue objects.

In life, what you focus on will tend to show up.

Also, what you focus your attention on grows, simply because you give it your energy. If you focus on red objects, you will see more red objects.

Think of something you wish to have. Let's say for example that you really fancy a pair of Nike trainers. The more you focus on the Nike trainers, the more you will tend to start seeing Nike trainers. In fact, you will start noticing them everywhere. Try it out! When you focus in your mind on an image which is important to you, your brain will start to notice that image when it presents itself in real life over and over again.

Further Activity

- Have one participant sit in the chair with his arms folded and slightly away from his chest.
- Select four other participants and have them stand two on either side of the seated participant.
- Two of the participants should stand beside the shoulders of the seated participant and two beside the knees of the seated participant.
- Have the standing participants interlock their own two hands together with their index fingers pointing out in front of them.
- On the count of three, have them place their index fingers under the right and left arm of the seated participant (just forward of the armpit area) and under the right and left knee of the seated participant respectively, and lift as hard as they can.
- They will not be able to lift the participant very high off the ground, if at all.

  Tip: if the participant is lifted off the chair with great ease, select a heavier participant.

- Now suggest to the participants that you are going to help them to focus their energies. Bring the four standing participants together and have them put their hands just above the head of the seated participant. Have them interlock their hands again and put them down in front of them. Tell them you are going to count to four. On the first three counts, have them take a deep breath and raise their hands above their head in a lifting motion, letting their breath out as they raise their hands. You will do this activity with them. Ask the seated participant to deep breathe along with them, and focus on feeling as light as a feather.

- On the fourth count, they are to stick their index fingers under the arms and knees of the seated participants and try again and lift with all their might. If the procedure is done correctly, the standing participants should be able to lift the seated participant off the chair quite easily.

  Tip: as they are going through the breathing and lifting simulation, the participants need to concentrate and not be distracted to be successful.

It is amazing what you can do if you focus your energies. The act of quiet concentration, even for a moment, harnesses the collective power of the body, mind and spirit.

Life Lesson/Skill

Remember that what you focus on in life, you tend to get. And what you focus on, grows. Focus on the things you wish to draw into your life, and this will tend to become a reality.

One evening, a Native American Chief was telling his tribe a story about two dogs that live in his mind.
One of the dogs he described as fearful and angry, the other courageous and joyful.

'These dogs are involved in a constant struggle,' he told them. One of the members of the tribe asked, 'Which dog wins?'

The Chief answered,
'The one I feed the most.'

Anonymous

36   Learning the Lesson

 Success is often as a result of good judgement. Good judgement is often as a result of experience. Experience is often as a result of bad judgement.

Anon

Toolbox

None.

Directions

- See below.

Activity

- Get the participants to think of a time when they 'lost' at something, or something didn't work out the way that they anticipated (or, if they are having difficulties thinking of a time, encourage them to draw a picture of that experience).
- Now ask them: 'What did you learn from that experience? What did that teach you?'

Explanation

There may be times in your life when you may feel that you have lost, or come second.

However, remember that while you may feel this way, it need not be a failure. There are only successes, and lessons. There is only true failure if you don't get the lesson.

If you 'lose', don't lose the lesson.

Thomas Edison was a man who learned that there is no such thing as failure, only lessons. It took him over 1,000 experiments before he invented the electric light bulb. On his thousandth experiment, after the fuse had exploded in a cloud of smoke once again, his apprentice asked him: 'Why do you keep trying when you have failed 1,000 times?'

Thomas Edison replied, 'Young man, I have not failed 1,000 times, I have simply discovered 1,000 ways that will not work, which brings me much closer to the one that will!'

Further Activity

- Get the participants to think again of the time when they 'lost' in their lives, or things didn't work out as they anticipated.
- Ask them, 'How will you act or perform differently next time?'
- Then get them to close their eyes and visualize themselves performing successfully next time. Encourage them to make the picture as big and bright as possible in their mind's eye, using colour, movement and sound.
- Alternatively, encourage them to picture in their minds a suitable hero/heroine. How would their hero/ heroine act if they lost a battle or things did not work as they anticipated?

Life Lesson/Skill

There will be times in your life when you may feel that you have 'lost'. If you 'lose', don't lose the lesson. There is always a lesson. Let it carry you forward towards your success.

Failure
is only
the opportunity
to begin again
more intelligently

Henry Ford

37 Feelings

> ❝ It is the way we react to circumstances that determines our feelings. ❞
> Dale Carnegie

Toolbox

Paper and pens/pencils as required.
A ball of string (optional).
A pair of scissors (optional).

Directions

- Hand a piece of paper and pen to each participant.

Activity

- Read out the situations from the first list on page 93 [situation list].
- After reading out each situation, ask the participants to write down a word which describes how they would feel in that situation.
- Encourage the participants to share the feelings described for each of the situations.
- Raise the following questions with the participants:
  o Did your feelings change in each situation?
  o Why do you think your feelings changed?
  o Did everyone feel the same about these situations?
  o Why did some participants feel differently to others?
  o How do you think feelings change?
  o What can be done to change your feelings about a situation?

Explanation

During the game, our feelings changed because the information we were given changed. In fact, it would be more accurate to say our feelings changed because our *thoughts* changed about the information we were given!

What we think about a particular situation will determine our feelings. If we have pleasant thoughts about a situation, we will tend to feel happy. Similarly, if we worry about a situation, we will tend to feel anxious. Our thoughts give rise to our feelings.

It follows from this if we want to change our feelings about a certain situation, we must change our thoughts about that situation.

Further Activity

- Ask for a volunteer.
- Have each of the other participants cut a piece of string and tie it to the arms, legs, wrists or fingers of the volunteer. Each participant is to hold a string.
- Read out the first situation given in the They Made Me Feel list on page 93. Encourage one of the participants to describe the feeling and pull on one of the strings.
- Each of the participants is to do the same, one by one.
- Now have the participants read out the situations at the same time, describe the feelings and pull on the strings at the same time.

Tip: this should be done gently to avoid injury!

Raise the following questions with the volunteer, for discussion with the other participants:

- How did it feel when other people were telling you how to feel in a certain situation?
- Did it feel like they were literally 'pulling your strings'?

- Was it possible to feel more than one way in the given situations?
- Did you have a choice as to how you felt?

Sometimes we are quick to say that, 'He or she makes me so angry.' But the truth is that no one can make you feel a certain way. *You* decide how you feel in any given situation.

Life Lesson/Skill

Our thoughts give rise to our feelings. If you want to change your feelings about a situation, begin by changing your thoughts. Remember that you decide how you feel in any given situation.

Situation List

1. You are riding your bike down the road when a child shouts, 'Hey you, don't steal my bike! Bring it back at once!' (describe feeling)

2. Then, as you stop and prepare to tell the child that the bike is your own, the kid examines the bike and says, 'Oh, I'm sorry. I thought the bike was mine. Mine is just like it. I just got one like it with money I have been saving for a year.' (describe feeling)
3. You are in a shop and a man nearly knocks you down as he runs out the door. (describe feeling)
4. A few moments later you hear someone say that his child has been knocked over by a car in the street. (describe feeling)
5. You are helping a friend of yours carry her books. By a mistake you drop them. She turns around and shouts at you, telling you what a clumsy fool you are. (describe feeling)
6. Later in the day your friend apologizes to you, saying that she was in a bad mood because she had studied hard for her maths test but had failed. (describe feeling)

They Made Me Feel

o Someone has stolen your favourite trainers.
o You didn't get invited to a friend's party.
o You failed a test.
o Your pet cat died.
o You got picked on because of a bad haircut.
o Your dad tells you he has lost his job.
o Your younger brother breaks your favourite toy.
o You have to go to the dentist to have a tooth pulled.

When you change your patterns of thinking, you change the way you feel about yourself, about others and about the world… Thinking is the gateway to our emotions, and emotions are the gateway to our actions.

Dr Arthur Freeman

38   **Sharing**

 No matter how little you have, you can always give some of it away.
Catherine Marshall

Toolbox

Several envelopes (optional).
Paper and pens (optional).

Directions

- None.

Activity

- Read the story on page 96 to the participants three times – first with Ending 1, then with Ending 2 and then with Ending 3.
- Dramatize the dialogue to emphasize the differences between the three approaches.
- Now read out the stories below and have the participants pick one story and choose three endings, each time including one where the characters avoid confrontation by sharing.
  - o Sarah and Simon are at home watching television. Each one wants to watch a different programme at the same time.
  - o Cathy and Claire are at the school fair. The art class is selling home-made chocolate brownies. Both reach for the last chocolate brownie at the same time.
  - o It's the first day of school and Lara wants to sit next to her best friend Annie, but all the desks around Annie are filled. She asks Frank to move, but Frank likes where he is sitting.
- Discuss with the participants how sharing does not only mean sharing good things together. It can also mean 'sharing the load' – helping one another to make a task easier.

Explanation

Sometimes we get caught up in ourselves and our own desires. In those moments we tend to focus only what is directly in front of us. We forget about giving.

Sharing is more than just giving something to someone else, however. When you share something of yours with another you contribute to their happiness. You allow them to experience something fun, joyful, exciting, tasty or nourishing!

Further Activity

- Reproduce the diagrams on page 97 either by hand or photocopy.
- Cut out the different pieces and write the letters on both sides of each piece.
- Label five envelopes A, B, C, D and E and place the pieces with the corresponding letters into that envelope. Envelopes A, B and C should each contain four pieces. Envelopes D and E should contain three pieces.
- Now sit five people around a table or on the floor.
- Distribute one envelope to each participant.
- Issue the following instructions to the participants:
  - o 'You will be given an envelope containing parts of squares. Between you there are enough pieces to make up five squares of equal size.
  - o The game is completed when the five squares have been completed.
  - o No person should have more than five pieces in front of them at any one time.
  - o You must not take pieces from another participant or signal for a piece to be given to you. You can only give pieces away to others.
  - o You must not talk or use sign language.'

Tip: if you want to play this game with just three participants, use just three squares. The number of participants should always match the number of squares.

In this game you have to be aware of the needs of those around you and share spontaneously in order to complete the squares successfully.

Try to be aware of those less fortunate than you. Do not be selfish. Share what you have with others openly and without resentment and you will usually find that they will do the same.

Life Lesson/Skill

Be gracious with others. Share what you have openly and without resentment. And as you give, so you will receive.

The Lego Story

Mike and Sean are playing with Lego. They are busy building a model. Oliver comes over and asks if he can join in.

Ending 1
Mike says, 'Okay.' Sean does not like Oliver very much and would prefer it if he didn't join them. Instead of saying anything, Sean just shrugs and carries on playing. Whenever Oliver makes a suggestion, Sean says that it's 'stupid'. Several times he snatches parts from Oliver without asking. After a few minutes, Oliver asks him if anything is the matter. Sean sighs and says, 'Nothing.'

Ending 2
Mike says, 'Okay,' but Sean says, 'No way!' Oliver asks, 'Why not?' Sean replies, 'I hate playing with you. You always act like you know everything. You don't listen, and you think your ideas are better than everyone else's.' Oliver shouts, 'You are a liar! You are just jealous because I am smarter than you are!' Sean becomes angrier now and shouts, 'You'd better leave before I make you!' 'Is that right?' Mike replies. Sean moves around the table towards Oliver, who flees to the other side of the room.

Ending 3
Mike says, 'Okay' but Sean says, 'No way!' Mike asks, 'Why don't you want Oliver to play with us?' Sean replies, 'Because I hate playing with him. He always acts like he knows everything. He doesn't listen and he thinks his ideas are better than everyone else's.' Oliver points out to Mike that he and Sean have been playing with the Lego for some time, and that they really belong to the class, not just to the two of them. Mike agrees with Oliver and offers to let Oliver work with him on the part of the model that he is building. Sean says, 'I guess that's okay, if you promise to listen to my ideas too.' Oliver answers, 'Sure, I'll listen to your ideas. And I will work on this side of the model with Mike. But if I have a suggestion about your part, can I ask you if it's okay to make it?' 'Sure,' Sean says.

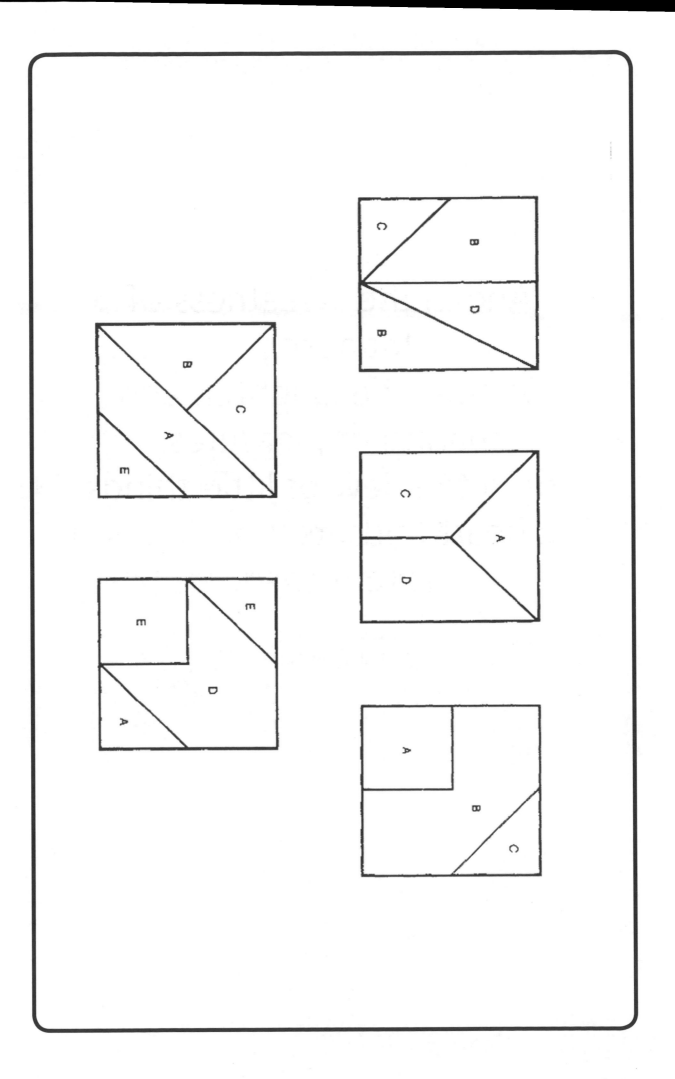

And in the sweetness of
friendship
let there be laughter, and
sharing of pleasures.
For in the dew of little things
the heart finds its morning and
is refreshed.

Kahlil Gibran

39   Word Power

 The words that enlighten the soul are more precious than jewels.
Hazrat Inayat Khan

Toolbox

Pad of paper and pens/pencils as required.
Sticky labels or name tags (optional).

Directions

- Hand a piece of paper and pen/pencil to each participant.
- Each participant should divide his page into two columns.

Activity

- In the left column each participant should write down a list of the things he does not like to do e.g. doing the dishes, homework, mowing the lawn, the long bus ride to school.
- Now in the right column, each participant should think of a way of describing that activity in a more empowering manner which makes it more attractive.
- For instance, you might change 'homework' to 'homeplay'; you might change 'long bus ride to the city' to 'journey to the city of dreams'; you might change 'doing the housework' to 'being a homemaker'; you might change 'tidying my room' to 'decorating my palace' etc.
- Try to think of as many crazy terms as possible with a prize for the winner!

Explanation

The words we use to describe things not only illustrate how we *do* feel about those things, but also to a large extent determine how we *will* feel about those things. If you describe something as a 'drag', that will usually be your experience – it becomes a 'drag', right?

We know that the words we use to describe things have a physical effect on the body. That is, they can affect the way the body reacts to those things (describe how a juicy orange tastes and notice what happens to your body as you do this!).

Imagine if a doctor described him/herself as a 'Healer of Souls', a teacher as 'a Miner of Human Potential', a financial advisor as a 'Wealth Creator', a mathematician as a 'Mental Magician' or a cook as a 'Culinary Genius'. Do you think they would feel more excited about their jobs? You bet they would.

Further Activity

- Get each participant to think of a positive alliterative adjective to preface his/her name e.g. Fabulous Fiona, Wonderful Wayne, Dynamic Dave, Terrific Tina etc.
- Continue until each participant has chosen an example. If a participant gets stuck, encourage the other participants to think of a name for that participant.
- Write the new names on a sticker for each participant.
- Now get each participant to sit in a circle and, in turn, shout out their new name with great gusto. You might ask each participant to accompany their description with a symbolic gesture. For example, Joyful John might open his arms and jump for joy.

Life Lesson/Skill

How we describe things to a large extent defines how we feel about them. Labels or words we use will affect the way we feel. For tasks which seem boring and tedious, change your description of the task and notice how it affects your attitude towards the task and your experience of it.

Language
exerts hidden power,
Like the moon
on the tides.

Rita Mae Brown

40 Preparation

 Before everything else, getting ready is the secret of success.
Henry Ford

Toolbox

Pad of paper and pen (optional).

Directions

- Have the participants stand in a circle. If there are more than ten participants, make two circles.
- Explain to them that the aim of this game is to have everyone sitting on the knees of the person behind them in the circle without it collapsing.

Activity

- When you say 'begin', have everyone sit down on the knees of the person behind them and try to support each other while retaining the shape of the circle.
- Without exact preparation, this activity will not succeed and the circle will collapse.
- Try again. This time, the participants should prepare properly. They should ensure that they are standing next to someone in the circle of approximately the same height. Secondly, they should ensure that their shoulders are aligned with the person in front of them, who will be sitting on their knees. Finally, everyone needs to sit down together at the exact same moment.

Explanation

The participants will find that this fun activity is impossible without proper preparation among the participants in the circle.

The 'P' Factor is a lesson which will serve you well in any endeavour in your life.

The 'P' Factor stands for 'Proper Preparation Prevents Poor Performance'.

When faced with an upcoming event, be it a presentation for class, an assignment, a dance show or a sports contest, remember to prepare properly. This will improve your performance without a doubt.

Further Activity

- Pair the participants into partners and have the partners face each other.
- Each participant should put their hands behind their back and extend any number of fingers on one or both hands.
- On the count of three, both participants are to bring their hands out in front of them. The first of the two people who correctly adds up the total of the number of fingers extended on his own hands and the hands of his partner shouts out the answer. The winner gets one point.
- Encourage each pair to have a couple of turns, before switching partners.
- The key to winning this game is to already know how many fingers you have extended on your own hands, so that when your partner extends his hands all you have to do is add his finger total to yours. Some simple preparation increases your chances of success greatly.
- Now get the participants to think of an event that is coming up in the future. If they can't think of an upcoming event, get them to think of a project they are working on.
- Encourage each participant to write down on a sheet of paper the main action steps that they will need to prepare for the event or project. Then, once they have identified what action steps they need to take, get them to write down how they will prepare for each action step to ensure that this is accomplished. Then get them to write down by which date each action will be accomplished.
- Are there any potential challenges they need to face in carrying out the event or project? If so, how will they best prepare for these challenges? Encourage the participants to brainstorm ways of dealing with the challenges ahead of time.
- Encourage the participants to think of a time when they did not perform well. Was it because of poor preparation? How could they have prepared better?

Life Lesson/Skill

Remember the 'P' Factor – Proper Preparation Prevents Poor Performance. If you prepare well for an upcoming event or project, you will reap the rewards.

It is better to be prepared for an opportunity and not have one, than to have an opportunity and not be prepared

Whitney Young, Jr.

Remember the 'P' Factor – Proper Preparation Prevents Poor Performance. If you prepare well for an upcoming event or project, you will reap the rewards.

102   50 Life Skills to Ensure Kids Stay Out of Trouble

41 Learning can be Fun

 The more you link, the more you learn.
Jeannette Vos

Toolbox

Your imagination.

Directions

- Make the announcement that today we are going to learn how to be world champion memorizers!

Activity

- We are going to memorize the nine planets in the Solar System, in order of distance from the Sun.
- First, get the participants to close their eyes.
- Now get them to picture the following sequence of images in their mind's eye:
  - o Approaching the front door of their house.
  - o Going inside and into the entrance hall.
  - o Going into their bedroom.
  - o Going over towards their bed.
  - o Opening their cupboard.
  - o Going into the bathroom and pulling back the shower curtain.
  - o Walking down the hallway or passageway.
  - o Sitting on the sofa in the living room.
  - o Going into the kitchen or laundry room and walking over to the washing machine.
- Ok, now get them to open their eyes.
- Announce that the nine planets are, in order, Mercury, Venus, Earth, Mars, Jupiter, Saturn, Uranus, Neptune and Pluto.
- Encourage the participants to once again close their eyes.
- Get them to imagine themselves standing outside the front door. Now get them to imagine that a great big red fireball comes hurtling through the front door, coming right past them – they have to jump out of the way! The red fireball represents Mercury.
- Now get them to go into the house and into the entrance hall. As they walk into the entrance hall, there walking towards them they see a beautiful princess with very long, blonde hair surrounded by giant floating hearts – that represents Venus, the Goddess of Love. Imagine the whole entrance hall filling up with giant floating hearts!
- They then move down the hall into their bedroom. As they open the bedroom door they see in front of them a giant pile of earth and a bulldozer moving the earth! They can barely get inside the room it is so big. That represents the planet Earth.

- Now get them to go over to the cupboard and open it. Out fall hundreds and hundreds of Mars bars, all over the room. There are so many big Mars bars just pouring out of the cupboard.
- Following this they go over to the bed. They should imagine that sitting on the bed in a large red robe and wearing a huge crown is the king of the gods, Jupiter. Encourage them to picture in their minds a large crown or wreath on his head. Get them to imagine bouncing on the bed with King Jupiter!

- Encourage them to imagine themselves walking into the bathroom. As they pull back the shower curtain or open the shower door, they see a clown juggling with giant rings. That represents the rings of Saturn, the next planet.
- Now get them to imagine that they are walking down the passage or hallway. As they walk, get them to imagine a giant 'U' in the middle of the hallway. Get them to climb up the giant 'U' and now slide all the way down the 'U', shouting in delight! This represents Uranus.
- Encourage them now to imagine themselves going into the living room and sitting on the sofa. As they sit down, get them to see a very large wave crashing through the windows, filling up the entire room with water and soaking them. This represents Neptune, the God of the Sea.
- Finally, get them to imagine themselves running out of the living room into the kitchen, taking off the wet clothes and putting them into the washing machine or dryer. As they do that, they see a large yellow object going round and round in the dryer. What could it be? As they stop the dryer and open up the machine, out bounds the dog Pluto!
- Do another quick journey through the house, picturing the huge red fireball (Mercury), the Goddess of Love and the floating hearts (Venus), the giant pile of earth (Earth), the falling Mars bars (Mars), the muscular King of the Gods sitting on this thrown (Jupiter), the clown juggling with the rings (Saturn), sliding down the 'U' (Uranus), the crashing wave filling up the living room (Neptune) and Pluto leaping out of the dryer.
- Now get the participants to open their eyes, and see if they can remember the order of the planets.

Explanation

We take in new information every day, don't we? But how can we remember all the information?

There are three keys to successful memorizing.

The first is using what's called *association*. Try to link an image in your mind or something you *do* know with the thing you are trying to remember.

Second, use your *imagination*. The more ridiculous and outrageous the image, the easier it will be to remember. Make the image big, colourful and of significance to you.

Third, use *locations* or *places*. The brain loves journeys. Using a journey that you know already (your house for example), store the images in a number of locations on that journey. You may have a journey to school that you do every day. If you are trying to memorize a list of 15 things, or key points, pick out 15 locations in order along the journey, starting with the bus stop, for example, and continuing until you get to the classroom.

These are the techniques used by many memory experts and by the author of this book in the World Memory Championships.

Unfortunately sometimes children have negative associations with learning. This may be because they have been taught in a boring way. For instance, simply writing down a long list of facts in sentences on the blackboard or on a printed sheet is most often not appealing to children and usually does not capture their imagination, one of the three essential keys to memory. If children use the three tools of association, imagination and location, as in the activity, they will find that learning can be easy and great fun![2]

Further Activity

- Encourage the participants to try out the techniques above for a school project. History is always a good example. If they are trying to remember 15 keys facts from the Second World War, get them to pick 15 locations in a journey they know well. First, get them to be clear on the locations. Then, get them to develop an image which represents each main fact. The images should be big, bright, coloured, moving and with sound if possible. Remember, the more outrageous the better!

Tip: getting the image to interact with the location also helps. For example, having the huge red fireball smash through the front door helps link the image to the location.

Life Lesson/Skill

We learn something new everyday. Learning can be fun and easy when using the right techniques.

42 Death and Dying

 What we think about death only matters for what death makes us think about life.
Charles de Gaulle, French President

Toolbox

A packet of balloons.

Directions

- Take one balloon out of the bag and demonstrate the activity below.

Activity

- Blow up one balloon in front of the participants.
- Hold it between your thumb and forefinger, explaining that initially the balloon was lifeless, until you filled it with air.
- Explain that the air that is inside the balloon is the same as the air on the outside – it is all part of the same universe.
- Now let the balloon go, watching it zoom around the room until it falls to the floor.
- Pick up the balloon again, explaining that the air that was inside the balloon has now passed out into the universe.
- Explain that the human soul – the most essential part of each of us – is like air, temporarily trapped inside the balloon (the body). On death, like the balloon, we change form. We no longer need our body. Our soul, like the air, is released again and becomes part of the universe.

Explanation

Children's questions about death are the hardest to answer. Teachers, parents and caregivers often avoid the subject altogether, either because they do not think it is their place to discuss the subject, they are uneasy with the subject themselves, or because they do not wish the children in their care to think about death, or, worse still, engage in discussions about death.

But the reality is that, regardless of your beliefs about what happens after death, death is a *part of life*. It is part of the circle of life. Indeed, all around us every day, we see birth and death, in a never-ending cycle.

After conducting extensive research, Sheila and Celia Kitzinger in their book *Talking with Children about Things that Matter* conclude:

 A vital element in coming to terms with the experience of death is talking about it.

Conversely, not talking about it can result in a child constructing his or own debilitating fears about death.

In America, the death of schoolteacher Christie McAuliffe, in the satellite launch of which she was the first civilian, was screened to millions of children. Similarly, in Britain, the death of Princess Diana was mourned extensively and publicly. Both of these events have prompted a controversial call for 'death education' in schools in America and Britain. Why? Because most parents today still do not talk about death with their children.

The game above has been shown to be a simple and effective way of introducing a subject which so affects our lives. It is not intended to be prescriptive or to promote a particular religion. The game is a suggestion and serves as a potential platform for discussion. It can also be adapted to fit different religious beliefs and the age of the relevant participants.

Further Activity

- In demonstrating the circle of life, take the participants outside to a tree which has a few leaves scattered beneath it on the ground.
- Pick up a leaf, or better still, watch as a leaf falls from the tree to the ground. When the leaf detaches itself

from the tree, it is unable to live. It is denied the lifeblood from the tree (the water and nutrients which pass from the roots up into the branches and out to the leaves). However, when it falls to the ground, it becomes compost. It enriches the soil once again and gives life to another tree. So the circle of life and death continues.

Life Lesson/Skill

Death is a part of life. Our bodies are like the balloon. They carry our soul. On death, we change form. Our soul, like the air, is released and becomes part of the universe.

One day Kisa Gotami came to Buddha crying, 'Oh Exalted One, my only son has died. I went to everyone and asked, "Is there no medicine to bring my son back to life?" And they replied, "There is no medicine; but go to the Exalted One, he may be able to help you." Can you, O Exalted One, give me medicine to bring my only son back to life?'

Looking at her with compassion, Buddha replied, 'You did well, Kisa Gotami, in coming here for medicine. Go, and bring me for medicine some tiny grains of mustard seed from every house where no one – neither parent, child, relative, nor servant – has died.'

Kisa Gotami, delighted in her heart, went away to fetch as many tiny grains of mustard seed as she could find. From one house to another, she searched frantically all day long, and each time she was told, 'Alas! Great is the count of the dead in this house.'

Overcome with exhaustion, she finally said, 'My dear little boy, I thought you alone had been overtaken by this thing which men call death. But now I see that you are not the only one, for this is a law common to all mankind.'

43

Choices

Every situation presents us with an opportunity to automatically react or consciously respond: a choice point…We are a product of our choices, not of our circumstances.
Eric Allenbaugh

Toolbox

Poster and pens/pencils as required.

Directions

- Photocopy the maze on page 108 and distribute.

Activity

- Encourage the participants to place the tips of their pens or pencils at the door of the maze and, without taking their pens or pencils off the page, try to find their way through the maze and out of the maze again.

Explanation

Throughout each day, and indeed throughout your life, you will be faced with choices. Life is much like a maze. Some turns that you take seem to end up nowhere. Others will lead you towards great joy and fulfilment. The decision to turn left or right, or go forward or back, has consequences.

You always have the power of choice. Sometimes you may feel that you have no choice. But in reality you do have the power to choose. Your greatest ability is the ability to choose your attitude or response to what happens around you in any given moment.

For example, Bob and Tim both get C's on their maths test. Bob decides that he is going to work harder next time and get a better grade. Tim decides that he is just no good at maths and gives up.

Alison and Kate both notice a new girl in class on Monday. When the bell goes, Alison keeps to herself. Kate goes over to say hello and makes a new friend.

Even when it appears as if you have taken a turn which ends up nowhere, something may come of it. You may find yourself exploring new territories that you never expected. Finally, remember that, as in the maze game, it is never too late to change your mind and change direction.

Further Activity

- Hold up the diagram on page 109 or copy the diagram onto a poster board. If you copy the diagram, do not let the participants see you drawing and cover up the diagram until you are ready to start the activity.
- Ask the participants to spend a couple of minutes counting the number of squares they see.
- Have the participant write the answers on a piece of paper and collect them. Read out the answers. Answers should range from 16 to 30.

Sometimes when we make a decision we look at one or perhaps two alternatives and make our choice from those. There are always a number of ways of looking at things. When making a decision or a choice, we need to remember to consider all the alternatives.

Life Lesson/Skill

The decisions you make every day do affect and determine where you end up. Remember you always have a choice. Your greatest ability is to choose your attitude in any given moment.

Here's Your Maze!

We who lived in the concentration camps can remember the men who walked through the huts comforting others, giving away their last piece of bread.

They may have been few in number, but they offer sufficient proof that everything can be taken away from a man except one thing:
the last of his freedoms –
to choose one's attitude
in any given set of
circumstances,
to choose one's own way.

Viktor Frankl

44 Compromise

 Compromise means that half a loaf is better than no bread.
G.K Chesterton

Toolbox

None.

Directions

- Divide the participants into pairs of roughly equal weight and height if possible.

Activity

- Have the participants face each other.
- The participants should put their feet together and ensure that their feet are touching each other, toe to toe.
- Propose that the participants should now clasp hands and lean backwards, trying to find the balancing point between them.

Explanation

Sometimes in order to complete a task successfully, we have to conduct a fine balancing act with another. There will need to be some give and take.

If one person is too demanding, or tries to 'throw his or her weight around', the required balance cannot be achieved and the project falls apart.

But with an awareness of the factors at play, and some careful adjustments, usually a suitable balance can be found to ensure that both parties achieve a favourable result.

This is usually called a compromise.

Further Activity

- Congratulations! Explain to the participants that they have just each won a fantastic holiday for two!
- Now divide the participants into pairs.
- Explain to the participants that there is only one condition to the holiday. They only have five minutes in which to select one of the designated holiday packages below. If they cannot reach a decision in five minutes, neither of them can go.
  o One week of doing nothing but lying on a beach in the sun and sleeping in hammocks;
  o One week at a secluded 5-star hotel in the mountains with full room service;
  o Two days in an average 3-star hotel in a party town with five of your best friends;
  o Three days at an exclusive spa including a full-body massage, aromatherapy treatment and jacuzzis;
  o Five day hike to see the gorillas in Central Africa but no luggage or extra clothing allowed;
  o Three-day visit to Disneyland with all rides free but you each have to take your parents;
  o Two weeks visiting the Kennedy Space centre and learning about space;
  o Five weeks in New York with a driver and a butler but only one of you can go;
  o One week shopping in Paris at all the leading fashion houses but you have to pay for what you buy out of your savings;
  o One week at a top African game reserve to see the last remaining White Lions of Timbavati but you have to have three vaccinations before you go;
  o Two weeks aboard the famous Trans-Siberian Express Train going across Eastern Europe and Asia, but no one speaks English on the train;
  o Five day cruise on a luxury Caribbean cruise liner with a group of 70 year olds;
  o One week assisting Aids orphans in a remote part of Zimbabwe planting food gardens.

Was it hard to reach a decision where each party was absolutely happy? Did you find that you ended up choosing a holiday which was not your first choice? How did that make you feel? Was it better than not going on the holiday at all? Discuss with the participants how they reached a compromise.

Reaching a compromise requires an awareness of the needs of others and the desire to reach a mutually beneficial agreement.

Read out the story The Tale of Three Kings below to the participants. Can you think of a country where this has really happened? What is the moral of the story?

Life Lesson/Skill

The ability to compromise when the situation requires it is a most useful and valuable skill. Reaching a compromise through working together is often the best way to achieve a favourable result.

The Tale of Three Kings

Once upon a time there lived three kings. Each king had a small kingdom. King Ho's kingdom was rich in food supplies. King Hee's land had the best fresh water. King Hum's kingdom had the best craftspeople.

King Ho said, 'I wish my kingdom was bigger. I'm really afraid that the barbarians from the north will come over the mountains and take my kingdom away from me.' 'Me too,' said King Hee. 'I know they need water. If they decide to take over my kingdom, I won't have the strength to stop them.' 'Neither will I,' said King Hum. 'I think we all have the same problem. The barbarians want what we have. By ourselves, we are not strong enough to keep them away, but together, we could be.'

King Ho said, 'What if we put our kingdoms together, and combine our resources such as our people, our food, our water, and our animals? We would be so strong the barbarians would never succeed in defeating us.'

King Hee and King Hum agreed that this was a good idea. But how would they manage to live together in harmony?

'We could share the rule of the kingdom by having a three-way ruling council,' said King Ho. 'We could vote on each important issue, and a two out of three vote would mean that the issue was agreed.'

'What if one of us didn't like the idea?' said King Hum.

'We would just have to go along with it anyway,' said King Ho.

'You mean I would not have complete control over my craftspeople?' gasped King Hum. 'And what if it didn't work out?' asked King Hee. 'I would have contributed all my precious water supplies.'

'Yes, but by giving up your precious water supplies, you would have gained plenty of nourishing food and skilled craftspeople,' said King Hum. 'And you would be safe from the dangerous barbarians.'

The kings could not agree. There was constant bickering about who would have to give up what. The barbarians, hearing about the kings' plan, gathered their forces at once and attacked while they could. They easily overcame each kingdom, one by one.

The law of win/win says,
'Let's not do it your way
or my way;

let's do it the best way.'

Greg Anderson

45

Drugs (Smoking)

 Smoking is a ghastly thing; blowing smoke out of our mouths into other people's mouths, eyes and noses, and having the same thing done to us!

Samuel Johnson

Toolbox

A balloon.
A rope to serve as a net.
Two chairs.
A number of drinking straws (optional).

Directions

- Blow up the balloon.
- Tie a rope between the tops of the two chairs so that it forms a net about 3 feet/1 metre off the ground.

Activity

- The participants are to lie on their backs facing the net.
- This game is played much like a volleyball game, except that participants are to remain on the floor at all times. Each team may hit the balloon three times before it must go over the net. If they do not succeed the other team gets a point. Participants should also rotate positions as in a normal volleyball game so that each participant gets to experience the different positions.

Tip 1: to make the game more challenging, you may wish to introduce more than one balloon into the game.
Tip 2: if there are a large number of participants, set up two games in different parts of the room.

Explanation

We use our lungs to breathe in the air that keeps us alive. Inside the air passage that leads to your lungs there are a number of fine hairs. These are known as cilia. The cilia protect the lungs from small particles of smoke and ash, so that you can breathe properly. The cilia wave backwards and forwards, pushing the particles back up to the mouth.

When a person smokes, the tar from the cigarette is inhaled and deposited on the cilia. Soon the cilia become covered in tar and can no longer perform their crucial waving action. When the waving action ceases, the tar moves through the passageway into the lungs. Over a period of time, the cilia stop functioning altogether and the body produces extra mucus to try to protect the lungs. This extra mucus builds up in the lungs and has to be coughed out by the smoker. This is what is known as 'smoker's cough'.

The balloons represent the particles of smoke or tar that pass down the air passage. The arms of the participants represent the cilia. To simulate the weakening of the cilia over time, have some participants play with one arm, or restrict each participant to one hit each. Any penalty or restriction will demonstrate your point of reduced cilia effectiveness.

Further Activity

- Have the participants stand up.
- Encourage each participant to close their nose with two fingers and take a few deep breaths in through the mouth.
- Now hand each participant a drinking straw. Repeat the process except that each participant is now to breathe only through the straw. Do not allow the activity to go on for so long that the participants feel faint. Just a few breaths will do (this exercise should be supervised).
- Each person has within their lungs a number of small sacks called alveoli. These small sacks allow the breathing process to work. When a person smokes a cigarette, he is inhaling tar into his lungs, as we

discussed above. Some of the tar that makes its way into the lungs becomes deposited onto these tiny sacks. The sacks become filled up with tar and stop functioning. Sometimes they can even burst. The result is that you have a reduced capacity to breathe. Your lungs cannot function properly. It is much like trying to breathe through a straw.

- Discuss with the participants the need to stay fit and healthy. Our bodies take care of us. We need to take care of our bodies too.

Life Lesson/Skill

As human beings, we need oxygen to survive. Smoking reduces the ability of our lungs to function properly. Without fully functioning lungs, we cannot breathe properly. And without breathing properly, we cannot get oxygen into our system.

46

Tidiness

 Life is too complicated not to be orderly.
Martha Stewart

Toolbox

List of items (as described below).
Pens or pencils for each participant.

Directions

- Arrange for a supervised trip to the local supermarket or nearby store.
- Draw up a list of a variety of items for the participants to find.
- Photocopy the list and ensure each participant has a copy.

Activity

- Tell the participants that they have to find the relevant items in a short space of time. The time limit imposed will vary according to the size of the group and the length of time available for the activity.
- Once they have located the item, each participant should tick off the item on the list and write down the price of that item.
- Once they have completed the list, get them to bring back the sheet of paper and hand it to you.
- Back in the classroom or at home, discuss tidiness. What is tidiness? When do things look tidy? When does one look tidy?
- Encourage recognition of some of the following elements of tidiness e.g. 'our room is tidy when everything is in its place', 'I am tidy when my shirt is tucked in or my hair is in place', 'the bookshelf is tidy when the books are stacked neatly on the shelf' etc.
- Discuss some of the reasons why it is important to tidy mentioned on page 118.

Explanation

A good quality or skill to develop is tidiness. Tidiness is really about having an order to things. Generally things don't work well when they are in a state of chaos, do they? Chaos causes confusion. It causes misunderstandings. Sometimes it causes accidents. On a very practical level, when things are in a state of chaos we battle to find what we are looking for.

Draw to the attention of the participants, either at the location or back in the room, that there is an order to things in the supermarket or store. Discuss how certain items that tend to go together are grouped together e.g. cleaning products. Discuss how each row of the supermarket usually has a board or sign indicating what is in that row. These procedures are put in place to ensure that people find what they are looking for easily and quickly.

Encourage the participants to imagine what it would be like if there was no order! What if the toothbrushes were next to the oranges but the boxes of toothpaste were next to the cereals?

The supermarket is a lot like life. We need to have an order to things. We need to keep things tidy and neat. We need to know where things are. Otherwise it's much harder to function properly.

Further Activity

- Inform participants that you are going to go on a 'Waste Walk' or a 'Tidiness Trip' around the school or home.
- For the 'Waste Walk', devise a trip around the school grounds. Encourage the participants to notice the waste or litter. Get them to use all of their senses in observing the waste e.g. observe the texture (smooth, rough, slippery, jagged etc.), sound (crinkling, silent etc.), smell (sharp, rotten, fragrant, sweet etc.), appearance (shape, shiny, colour etc.).
- What makes the grounds untidy?
- Where does the rubbish come from? How did it get there? Did it come from school lunches? Are people

dropping it on the ground? Did it blow out of bins? Are there enough bins? Do the bins have lids? What can be done to reduce the waste and make the grounds tidier?

- What are the consequences for the school if the level of waste increases?
- Take the participants to meet the caretaker. Ask the caretaker to explain what his or her role is at the school. Discuss ways in which the participants can help the caretaker with his or her job.
- For the 'Tidiness Trip' around the home, discuss on your journey the concept of recycling and the benefits to the environment. Assist in making up special boxes or cartons for certain types of waste for recycling if your neighbourhood has a recycling programme.

Tidiness is not just a good idea that may earn you extra pocket money or a gold star. It has real practical advantages. Without order we would not be able to drive on the roads, make a meal or shop in a supermarket. Keeping things clean and tidy also enables us to live in a healthy and safe environment.

Life Lesson/Skill

We need to keep things tidy and neat. We need to have order to things. We need to know where things are. Keeping things clean, tidy and in good order enables us to live in a healthy and safe environment.

WHY DO WE TIDY?

1. Efficiency – it is quicker and easier to find things.

2. Safety – we will not trip and fall over things if they are put away.

3. Protection – things will not get damaged and will last longer.

4. Visually – our room looks better.

5. Health – our rooms can be cleaned more easily, making for a healthier environment.

47 Spreading Rumours

> A cruel story runs on wheels, and every hand oils the wheels as they run.
> Ouida

Toolbox

None.

Directions

- Arrange for the participants to stand in a circle.

Activity

- Each participant should take it in turn to slowly walk around in the middle of the circle.
- As the participant walks around, encourage the participants in the circle to whisper nasty rumours about the participant as he walks around. Some may be encouraged to snigger and giggle.
- After the game, ask each participant to recount what it felt like when rumours were being spread about them.

Tip: if the group of participants is very large, divide the group in subgroups for this game.

Explanation

What are rumours? Rumours are statements which have not been verified by those making them. They are usually made behind someone's back or out of earshot.

We have probably all been in the situation at some point where other people have spread false rumours about us. Nobody likes to be the subject of rumours. Spreading a false rumour is unfair on the person who is the subject of the rumour. Firstly, saying something negative about someone behind their back is not a very nice thing to do. Secondly, the relevant person is not there to defend himself against the rumour.

Further Activity

- Encourage the participants to play the old game known as 'Telephone' or 'Broken Telephone'.
- Have the participants sit in a long line.
- Formulate a false rumour about nobody in particular and tell the rumour to the first person in the row, asking them to pass the rumour on along the row.
- When the rumour reaches the last person in the row, get the last person to say it out loud.
- Discuss how the rumour has developed and changed. Discuss the damage a false rumour can cause to someone. Engage the participants in a debate about what to do when they are asked to participate in spreading a rumour.

A rumour changes and develops as it moves from one person to another. The result is that it can become even more damaging for the person concerned.

Life Lesson/Skill

When a rumour spreads, it takes on a life of its own. It rapidly changes and develops as it moves from one person to another. False rumours can be very damaging to a person. Try not to participate in spreading rumours. Rather take steps to find out the truth yourself.

50 Life skills

GAMES FOR AGES 9 AND UPWARDS

48

Positive Thinking

' Sow a thought, reap an action,
Sow an action, reap a habit,
Sow a habit, reap a character,
Sow a character, reap a destiny.'
Anthony Robbins

Toolbox

None.

Directions

- At least two participants are required. If there are more than two participants, divide the participants up into pairs.

Activity

- Person A should stand up, with his arms at the side and his eyes closed.
- Person A will then lift one arm up to the side and hold it parallel to the ground, making his arm as stiff as a plank.
- Person B will place his palm on the wrist of the extended arm and attempt to push the arm downwards firmly.
- Person A is to resist against B's downward pressure.
- Now have Person A say out loud 'I am [add their name]' while Person B pushes down on his arm. Person B tests the resistance level while Person A makes the statement.
- Person A then does the exercise again except this time repeating someone else's name (in other words, lying) e.g. 'I am [John Smith]'. Person B tests the resistance level while Person A makes the statement again.
- Finally, get Person A to close their eyes and hold a picture in their mind of someone they don't like and do the muscle test again. Then get them to hold a picture in their mind of someone they do like and repeat the testing.

Explanation

Thoughts may seem to be just ideas. However, scientists have proven that each thought has a physical effect on the body. Every thought that a person has produces an electrical current in the body which affects the strength of the muscles in the body (this is known as kinesiology).

The thought that you hold in your mind at any one time will therefore have a corresponding effect on the ability of the body to perform effectively.

When Person A spoke the truth, he tested strong (the arm stayed firm). However, when he made a false statement, he tested weak (the arm was unable to resist and was pushed downwards easily). This is the same for positive thoughts. Positive thoughts about things or people will make your muscles test strong. Negative thoughts will weaken your muscles.

It is important therefore not to spend any time on negative thoughts. Try not to be anxious or worried. Try not to think negative thoughts about people. Think positive thoughts wherever possible.

Your thoughts determine the very nature of the person you become. In fact, the quality of your life will be largely dependent on the quality of your thoughts.

Tip: ensure that partners swap so that each person can experience this for himself.

Further Activity

- Announce to the participants that you are now going to play the 'Fortunately…Unfortunately' game.
- Have the participants divide into pairs.

- Person A will begin by making a statement beginning with 'unfortunately' e.g. 'Unfortunately, I had to help my father mow the lawn today.'
- Person B will reply by making a related statement beginning with 'fortunately' e.g. 'Fortunately, the grass was not long so it was done very quickly.'
- Person A can continue with the same topic or use a different topic, each time beginning with 'unfortunately' and Person B countering with 'fortunately'.
- Persons A and B should then swap so that the roles are reversed.

Every cloud has a silver lining, as the saying goes. If you try hard enough, you will find the positive in most situations. Sometimes we allow ourselves to get into the habit of thinking negatively. Positive thinking is also a habit and requires practice. The above activity helps us to practise seeing the positive in situations that confront us on a day-to-day basis.

Life Lesson/Skill

Know and understand that every thought has a physical effect on the body. Our thoughts affect how we feel about things. Every thought will affect our muscles, the way we move and our performance. Therefore, try at all times to think positive thoughts about people and situations.

A pessimist sees the difficulty in every opportunity.

An optimist sees the opportunity in every difficulty.

Sir Winston Churchill

49 Relationships

 Nine-tenths of wisdom is appreciation. Go find somebody's
hand and squeeze it, while there's time.
Dale Dauten

Toolbox

Pad of paper and pens/pencils as required.

Directions

- Hand out a piece of paper and pen/pencil to each participant.

Activity

- The participants are now going to take a short quiz!
- Here are the questions:
  o Question 1 – Name five current prime ministers.
  o Question 2 – Name five Olympic gold medallists.
  o Question 3 – Name five Oscar winners for best actress or actor.
  o Question 4 – Name five winners of the MTV Best New Artist Award.
  o Question 5 – Name five Nobel Prize winners.
- These questions are not easy to answer, are they?
- Now get the participants to answer the following questions:
  o Question 1 – List five teachers who have aided your journey through school.
  o Question 2 – Name three friends with whom you play regularly or who have helped you in a difficult time.
  o Question 3 – Name five people who have taught you something worthwhile.
  o Question 4 – Think of five people who made you feel appreciated.
  o Question 5 – Think of five people you enjoy spending time with.

Explanation

The first quiz was pretty tough, right? These people are no second-rate achievers. They are the best in their fields. But we struggle to remember the headliners of yesterday. The applause dies. Awards are forgotten. Medals and certificates are buried with their owners.

The lesson is that the people who make a difference in your life are not the ones with the most credentials, the most money, the most fame, or the most awards. They are the ones that *care*. These are the ones we remember, and should acknowledge.

Tip: you may need to change the first set of questions depending on the age of the participants. But remember that they are designed to be hard!

Further Activity

- Get each participant to think of a person who makes a real difference in their life – perhaps someone whom they have not seen or spoken to for a while. Take 15 minutes and encourage them to write a letter to that person letting them know they make a real difference.

Life Lesson/Skill

At the end of the day, the people who make a real difference in your life are the ones that care. Take time to acknowledge the people who make a difference in your life.

Let us
be grateful
to people
who make us happy;
they are the
charming gardeners
who make our
soul blossom.

Marcel Proust

50 *Life skills*

GAMES FOR AGES 10 AND UPWARDS

50

Drugs (Alcohol)

 Alcohol is a good preservative for everything but brains.
Mary Pettibone Poole

Toolbox

A pair of sunglasses (optional).
A tube of Vaseline (optional).
At least three balloons (optional).

Directions

- Divide the participants up into pairs.
- Choose one participant to be Person A and the other to be Person B.

Activity

- Person A places his arms straight out in front of him parallel to the floor, with the palms facing each other.
- Now have Person A cross his arms over each other with his arms still out straight, forming an 'X' shape.
- Person A now turns the palms inwards so that they face each other again and interlocks his fingers.
- Person A pulls the hands in towards the body by going in a downward motion and bringing them up underneath his chin.
- Person B is now to ask Person A to move different fingers. Person B is to point to a finger quickly and say, 'Move this one', but not to actually touch the finger he wants moved. Person B should not allow much time between requests.
- Now have the participants switch roles.

Tip: to make this easier, have Person B actually touch the finger he wants moved.

Explanation

Most participants find it hard to move the correct fingers. Why is this? Why is the message not getting through to the brain?

By crossing the arms over and then pulling the hands up under the chin, you are confusing the brain. The brain is 'wired' so that the right side of the brain controls the left side of the body, and the left side of the brain controls the right side of the body.

When you cross your hands, the eyes cannot quickly tell the brain which finger to move!

When you drink alcohol, the same thing happens. You think the task looks easy. But your reactions are slowed, and you make mistakes. The message does not get through to the brain quickly. And when it does eventually get through, the brain easily makes an error of judgement.

Further Activity

- Blow up the balloons.
- Surreptitiously rub a small amount of Vaseline in a circular motion on the sunglasses.
- Give two balloons to a participant and ask him to keep bouncing them in the air so that they do not hit the ground. Introduce another balloon. He should be successful with two balloons but three should be challenging.
- Collect the balloons and explain that now the participant is going to experience what it is like to be under the influence of alcohol.
- Hand the sunglasses to the participant and encourage them to try the same exercise whilst wearing the sunglasses.

Tip: the more participants and balloons you have, the more the confusion is heightened and the harder it is to concentrate.

Under the influence of alcohol, your senses become less effective. Your vision is blurred and it is difficult to act quickly and precisely, much like the experience in the balloon game.

You may wish to use the above activities as a basis for a discussion around the potential consequences of being under the influence of alcohol.

Life Lesson/Skill

While these games are fun, remember that drinking alcohol is not a game. Alcohol confuses the brain and slows down the senses, causing you to make simple mistakes.

ANSWERS

Solutions for Activity 34

Dots activity

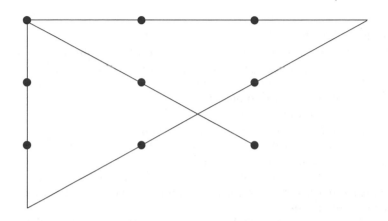

Uses for a paper clip

1.   You could use a paper clip to fasten a torn piece of clothing together.
2.   You could use it to eat sushi.
3.   You could use it as a nose clip when taking out the garbage.
4.   You could clip it on your ear as an earring.
5.   You could use it to fasten a necklace together.
6.   You could use it to hang car keys.
7.   You could use it to scratch yourself.
8.   You could use it to write in the sand.
9.   You could use it to turn a screw.
10. You could use it as a skewer to cook food over a fire.
11. You could use it for cleaning fingernails.
12. You could use it as an imaginary friend.
13. You could use it as a reminder to do something.
14. You could use it to strum a guitar.
15. You could use it to clean out the holes in the salt pot.
16. You could use it to pop a balloon.
17. You could use it in a game of tiddlywinks.
18. You could use it to pick a lock.
19. You could use a HUGE paper clip as a sled.
20. You could melt down a HUGE paper clip and pour it into a giant mould to make an iron broach.
21. If you were a warrior, you could use a large paper clip as a weapon.
22. If you were a ballerina, you could use a HUGE paper clip as a practice bar in the studio.
23. If you were a surfer, you could use a giant paper clip as a surfboard.
24. If you were a singer, you could use a giant paper clip as a microphone stand.
25. If you were a scientist, you could use a tiny paper clip to hold in place a small insect under a microscope.
26. If you were a painter, you could use a paper clip as a paintbrush.
27. You could have a paper clip as a pet (in the same way that people have pet stones!)
28. You could use it to clip negatives up under a light.
29. A mouse could use it as a javelin.
30. A monkey could use it to dig fleas out of his ear.
31. A naughty child could use it to flick chewing gum.

32. A magician could use it in a trick.
33. A fly could use it to jump-start its flight.
34. An ant could use it as a lookout.
35. A squirrel could use it to mark his buried acorns.
36. A beetle could use it to sail down a stream.
37. You could mess up a filing system by removing all the paper clips!
38. You could make a pair of spectacles or glasses with some large paper clips.
39. You could use a paper clip to make decorative patterns on a cake.
40. You could use a large paper clip as a kite.

Associations between 40 objects and a coat hanger

1. **Tennis Ball** The coat hanger could be bent to form a scoop for picking up tennis balls, or as a frame for a small racket, in order to hit a tennis ball.
2. **Rain** By lashing material around it, your coat hanger could form a primitive umbrella to protect you from the rain.
3. **Medal** Turn the coat hanger upside down and you can hang your medal from it.
4. **Telephone** A coat hanger could be used to pick up the receiver.
5. **Shell** The coat hanger would be an ideal cleaner for the shell.
6. **Guitar** The coat hanger can be used for strumming the guitar.
7. **Clown** The coat hanger could be used as one of a series of items with which the clown could juggle.
8. **Foot** The coat hanger could be used as a foot scratcher.
9. **Potato** The coat hanger could be used to punch holes in the potato before you microwave it.
10. **Handkerchief** Tie the handkerchief to the end of an unravelled coat hanger to make a flag, or tie it to all the sides and use it to filter water.
11. **Hat** Fix some material across the hanger and use it as a hat to shield you from the sun.
12. **Onion** Use the coat hanger to peel back the layers of the onion.
13. **Plant** A coat hanger can be used as a support for the growing plant.
14. **Pencil** Use the coat hanger to write in sand or clay or on wood.
15. **Planets** Use your coat hanger to hang models of the planets from the ceiling.
16. **Fork** The coat hanger can be used as a fork to pick up food.
17. **Coffee** The coat hanger can be used to stir your cup of coffee before you drink it.
18. **Watch** A coat hanger can be used to make a sundial, which you can use to tell the time.
19. **Ice** The coat hanger can be used to cut ice blocks.
20. **Kangaroo** Mould the coat hanger into the shape of a kangaroo, or bounce it on the ground like a bouncing kangaroo!
21. **Cereal Bowl** Use the coat hanger to scrape those last bits of cereal out of the box.
22. **Flashlight** Melt the coat hanger and use the metal to make a flashlight.
23. **Pepper** Use a heavy coat hanger to break the peppercorns.
24. **Wig** The coat hanger can be used to groom the hairs on the wig!
25. **Bell** Bang the coat hanger against the bell to ring it.
26. **CD** Thread the coat hanger through the middle of the CD and use it as a CD holder.
27. **Oak Tree** Use the coat hanger to search for acorns so as to plant a new oak tree.
28. **Tortoise** Stroke the tortoise gently on its shell with the coat hanger.
29. **Goat** Use a bunch of coat hangers to construct a fence for your pet goat!
30. **Singing** The coat hanger can be used as a triangle.
31. **Surfboard** Use the coat hanger as a leash to wrap around your foot.
32. **Eagle** The coat hanger could be used as a perch for the eagle.
33. **Hot-air Balloon** The coat hanger could be used to pop the hot-air balloon.
34. **Cowboy** The coat hanger can be melted and used to make a bullet for a six-gun.
35. **Telescope** Use the coat hanger to create a stand upon which to rest your telescope.
36. **Carpet** Use the coat hanger to scrape up the bits and pieces of dirt on a carpet.
37. **Sun** Using the light of the sun, allow the coat hanger to cast shadows in the form of animals against a wall or sheet.
38. **Saw** Use the coat hanger as a saw to cut through a big slab of butter or cake.
39. **Cardigan** A coat hanger could be used as a knitting needle to knit a cardigan.
40. **Yacht** A coat hanger could be used as a rudder or a small sail.

BIBLIOGRAPHY

Badegruber, B. (2006), *101 Life Skills Games for Children*. Hunter House Publishers.

Bond, T. (1986), *Games for Social and Life Skills*. Stanley Thornes (Publishers) Limited.

Buzan, T. (2001), *The Power of Spiritual Intelligence*. Thorsons.

—(2000), *Head First*. Thorsons.

—(2001), *Head Strong*. Thorsons.

—(2003), *Mind Maps for Kids*. Thorsons.

Canfield, J. and Hansen, M. V. (1995), *Chicken Soup for the Soul* (revised edn). Health Communications.

—(1996) *A 3rd Serving of Chicken Soup for the Soul*. Health Communications.

Cassingham, R. (1999), *The Best of Heroic Stories – Volume 1*. Freelance Communications.

—(1999), *The Best of Heroic Stories – Volume 2*. Freelance Communications.

Ciardiello, S. (2003), *Activities for Group Work with School-Age Children*. Marco Products.

Covey, S. (1990), *The Seven Habits of Highly Effective People*. Simon & Shuster.

Dryden, G. and Vos, J. (2001), *The Learning Revolution*. Network Educational Press.

Dubois, S. and Knight P. (1995), *Group Activities for Personal Development*. Speechmark Publishing Limited.

Einan, D. (2004), *Things to Do to Play and Learn*. Octopus Publishing Group.

Jackson, T. (1993), *Activities that Teach*. Red Rock Publishing.

Keenan, B. (1993), *An Evil Cradling*. Vintage.

Kehoe, J. and Fischer N. (2002), *Mindpower for Children*. Zoetic Inc.

Kitzinger S. and Kitzinger, C. (2000), *Talking with Children About Things That Matter*. Rivers Oram/Pandora.

Koehler, M. and Royer, K. (2001), *First Class Character Education Activities Program*, Prentice Hall.

Mannix, D. (2002), *Character Building Activities for Kids*. Jossey-Bass.

Martenz, J. (2001), *Character Building Classroom Guidance*. Marco Products.

McElherne, L. N. (1999), *Jump Starters*. Free Spirit Publishing.

Miller, J. (1998), *10-Minute Life Lessons for Kids: 52 Fun and Simple Games and Activities to Teach your Children*. Harper Perennial.

Mosley, J. and Sonnet, H. (2002), *101 Games for Self Esteem*. LDA.

Pelzers, D. (2001), *Life Lessons*. Element.

Peyser, S. and McLaughlin M. (1997), *Character Education Activities for K-6 Classrooms*. Educational Media Corp.

Robbins, A. (1991), *Unlimited Power* (reissue edn). Ballantine Books.

—(1992), *Awaken the Giant Within: How to Take Immediate Control of Your Mental, Emotional, Physical and Financial Destiny* (reprint edn). Free Press.

Schilling, D., Cowan, D. and Parlomares, S. (2000), *Leadership 2000: Preparing Students for Success and Leadership in the Workplace*. Innerchoice Publishing.

Schrumpf, F., Freiburg, S. and Skadden, D. (1993), *Life Lessons for Young Adolescents: An Advisory Guide for Teachers*. Research Press.

Sharma, R. (1999), *The Monk Who Sold his Ferrari*. HarperCollins.

Sher, B. (1998), *Self Esteem Games*. John Wiley and Sons, Inc.

Smith, M. (1993), *What's Up? – A Solution Guide for Today's Young People*. Success by Choice.

Stockwell, T. (1993), *Flyer Learning Activities*. EFFECT (European Foundation for Education, Communication and Teaching).

—(undated), *50 Non-prepared Learning Activities*, EFFECT.

Unell, B. C. and Wyekoff, J. L. (1995), *20 Teachable Virtues: Practical Ways to Pass on Lessons of Virtue and Character to Your Children*. Berkeley Publishing Group.

Vernon, A. (1989), *Thinking, Feeling, Behaving: An Emotional Education Curriculum for Children*. Research Press.

Weston, D. C, and Playwise, M. S. (1996), *365 Fun-filled Activities for Building Character, Conscience and Emotional Intelligence in Children*. Jeremy P. Tarcher/Putnam Books.

Zientek, J. (2001), *Mrs Ruby's Life Lessons for Kids*. Marco Products Inc.

REFERENCES

Chapter 1: Tolerance
Apple game adapted from *10-Minute Life Lessons for Kids* by J. Miller, p. 48.

Chapter 2: Sticking Together
Stick game adapted from the film *The Straight Story*, directed by David Lynch and written by John Roach and Mary Sweeney. With thanks to Jay Sauerbrei.

Chapter 3: Honesty
Yarn game adapted from Children's Ministry online magazine, July/August edn, published on www.cmmag.com
Bleach game adapted from *10-Minute Life Lessons for Kids* by Miller, J., p. 86.

Chapter 4: Trust
Falling game taken from Tony Quinn's *Educo* seminar.
Blindfold Walk adapted from *Group Activities for Personal Development* by S. Dubois and P. Knight, p. 25.

Chapter 5: The Power of Visualization
Jumping game adapted from *Mind Power for Children* by J. Kehoe and N. Fischer, p. 56–7.
Pointing game taken from Anthony Robbins' seminar *Unleash the Power Within*.

Chapter 6: Self-confidence
Karate-chop game adapted from *10-Minute Life Lessons for Kids* by J. Miller, p. 133.
What Would You Do If? adapted from *10-Minute Life Lessons for Kids* by J. Miller, p. 176.

Chapter 9: Goal Setting
The Jar of Fleas story adapted from *Leadership 2000: Preparing Students for Success and Leadership in the Workplace* by D. Schilling, D. Cowan and S. Parlomares, p. 214.

Chapter 10: Challenges
Carrot, egg and coffee bean story could not be traced to any particular author, despite extensive efforts. Parable of the Mule adapted from *First Class Character Education Activities Program* by Michael D. Koehler and Karen E. Royer, p. 133. For the complete parable, see 2nd International Pow-Wow events, Ranger Net Home, Official Royal Rangers website, www.rangernet.org

Chapter 11: Miracles
The author has made every attempt to trace the author of the piece Miracles, but has been unsuccessful to date. The story has been circulated on the internet as a true story, however no one has been successful in tracing the surgeon Dr Carlton Armstrong as yet. See www.truthminers.com or www.snopes.com/glurge/price.htm
Selected information on human body taken from Tony Buzan's book *Head Strong*, p. 148.

Chapter 12: Teamwork
Flying in a 'V' Formation adapted from a story by Angeles Arrien, who wrote it for Outward Bound, 1991. Also referred to in a story called *The V Formation of Bird Migration* by Lisa Shea.

Chapter 13: Gratitude
Because game adapted from *First Class Character Education Activities Program* by Michael D. Koehler and Karen E. Royer, p. 350.

Chapter 14: Judgement
Jumping Note game adapted from *Activities that Teach* by T. Jackson, p. 122.

Chapter 15: Expressing Feelings
Balloon game adapted from *Activities for Group Work with School-Age Children* by S. Ciardiello, p. 42.
Paper Bag game adapted from *Thinking, Feeling, Behaving* by A. Vernon, p. 33.

Chapter 16: Listening
Number game adapted from *101 Games for Self-Esteem* by J. Mosley and H. Sonnet, p. 115.
Blindfold game adapted from *Self Esteem Games* by B. Sher, p. 76.

Chapter 18: Contribution
Starfish Parable used with acknowledgement to 'The Starfish Greathearts Charitable Foundation'.

Chapter 20: Persistence and Practice
List of incredible achievements adapted from *A Third Serving of Chicken Soup for the Soul* by Jack Canfield and Mark Victor Hansen, p. 283, and *Head Strong* by Tony Buzan, p. 140.

Chapter 21: Questions
Six Power Questions taken from Anthony Robbins' 'Life Mastery' seminar manual.

Chapter 22: The Senses
Blindfold game with acknowledgement to Rebecca Bukenya.

Chapter 23: Stress
Breathing and Visualization Experience adapted from *50 Activities for Teaching Emotional Intelligence* by D. Schilling, p. 65.

Chapter 25: Disabilities and Weaknesses
Name One Good Thing and One Bad Thing game adapted from 'I Can, I Can't' game as illustrated in *101 life skills games for children* by Bernie Badegruber, p. 18.

Chapter 28: Labels
Tin game adapted from *Games for Social and Life Skills* by T. Bond, p. 71.
Camping Trip game adapted from *Games for Social and Life Skills* by T. Bond, p. 66.

Chapter 29: Communication
Ball and Coin game adapted from *Activities that Teach* by T. Jackson, p. 207.
South Pole game adapted from *Games for Social and Life Skills* by T. Bond, p. 147.

Chapter 30: Compassion
Shoe game adapted from *Jump Starters* by L. McElherne, p. 44.
Newspaper game adapted from *Thinking, Feeling, Behaving* by A. Vernon, p. 197.
Parable of the Stone adapted from the story 'Precious Gift' on the website www.spiritual.com.au

Chapter 31: Creativity
Top 10 Creative Rules of Thumb adapted from that compiled by Charles Chic Thompson as published on www.quoteland.com

Chapter 33: Peer Pressure
Saying 'No' game adapted from *Activities that Teach* by T. Jackson, p. 129.
Egg game adapted from *Activities that Teach* by T. Jackson, p. 210.

Chapter 34: Thinking Outside the Box
Paper clip game adapted from Tony Buzan's book *Head First*, p. 25.

Chapter 35: Focus
Focus game taken from Anthony Robbins' seminar *Unleash the Power Within*.
Lifting game adapted from *Activities that Teach* by T. Jackson, p. 177.

Chapter 37: Feelings
Thinking/Feeling game adapted from *Thinking, Feeling, Behaving* by A. Vernon, p. 103.
They Made Me Feel game adapted from *Thinking, Feeling, Behaving* by A. Vernon, p. 187.

Chapter 38: Sharing
Three Endings game adapted from *50 Activities for Teaching Emotional Intelligence* by D. Schilling, p. 119.
Squares game adapted from *Games for Social and Life Skills* by T. Bond, p. 216.

Chapter 39: Word Power
New Name game adapted from *101 Games for Self-Esteem* by J. Mosley and H. Sonnet, p. 61.

Chapter 40: Preparation
Numbers game adapted from *Activities that Teach* by T. Jackson, p. 119.

Chapter 42: Death and Dying
Balloon game adapted from *Talking with Children about Things that Matter* by Sheila Kitzinger and Celia Kitzinger, p. 191.

Chapter 43: Choices
Squares game adapted from *Activities that Teach* by T. Jackson, p 100.

Chapter 44: Compromise
Dream Holiday game adapted from *Games for Social and Life Skills* by T. Bond, p. 220. 'The Tale of the Three Kings' adapted from *Character Building Classroom Guidance* by J. Martenz, p. 143.

Chapter 45: Drugs (Smoking)
Balloon Volleyball game adapted from *Activities that Teach* by T. Jackson, p. 104.
Straw game adapted from *Activities that Teach* by T. Jackson, p. 149.

Chapter 46: Tidiness
'Why do we Tidy?' poster page and 'Waste Walk' idea adapted from The Keep Christchurch Beautiful Campaign: School Resource for Years 1–3, published by Christchurch City Council, Christchurch, New Zealand in 2002.

Chapter 47: Spreading Rumours
Rumour game adapted from that used in *101 life skills games for children* by Bernie Badegruber, p. 136.

Chapter 48: Positive Thinking
Fortunately…Unfortunately game adapted from *Self Esteem Games* by B. Sher, p. 163.

Chapter 49: Relationships
Question game credited to Charles (Peanuts) Schultz.

Chapter 50: Drugs (Alcohol)
Balloon game adapted from *Activities that Teach* by T. Jackson, p. 80.

END NOTES

1 A child may have global beliefs about the world in general which are limiting/negative (e.g. life is hard, people are mean, the world is doomed). These can be replaced with more empowering beliefs (e.g. life is rewarding for those who work hard, people are inspirational, the world is full of opportunity). Similarly, a child may have personal beliefs which are negative/limiting (e.g. I am a lousy athlete, I can't do maths, I am ugly) which can be replaced with more empowering beliefs (e.g. I am getting fitter and stronger every day I work out, I can do maths, I am beautiful).

2 Kids should be encouraged to use Mind Maps® when learning as well. A Mind Map® is a fun tool developed by Tony Buzan using the exact three principles outlined above: association, imagination and location. Mind Maps® also help people use both sides of their brain – the left and right cerebral hemispheres. For more on this, read *Mind Maps for Kids* by Tony Buzan.